STARTING WITH ROUSSEAU

Continuum's *Starting with . . .* series offers clear, concise and accessible introductions to the key thinkers in philosophy. The books explore and illuminate the roots of each philosopher's work and ideas, leading readers to a thorough understanding of the key influences and philosophical foundations from which his or her thought developed. Ideal for first-year students starting out in philosophy, the series will serve as the ideal companion to study of this fascinating subject.

Available now:

Starting with Berkeley, Nick Jones

Starting with Derrida, Sean Gaston

Starting with Descartes, C. G. Prado

Starting with Nietzsche, Ullrich Haase

Forthcoming:

Starting with Hegel, Craig B. Matarrese

Starting with Heidegger, Thomas Greaves

Starting with Hobbes, George Macdonald Ross

Starting with Hume, Charlotte R. Brown and William Edward Morris

Starting with Kant, Andrew Ward

Starting with Kierkegaard, Patrick Sheil

Starting with Leibniz, Lloyd Strickland

Starting with Locke, Greg Forster

Starting with Merleau-Ponty, Katherine Morris

Starting with Mill, John R. Fitzpatrick

Starting with Sartre, Gail Linsenbard

Starting with Schopenhauer, Sandra Shapshay

Starting with Wittgenstein, Chon Tejedor

STARTING WITH ROUSSEAU

JAMES DELANEY

continuum

Continuum International Publishing Group
The Tower Building   80 Maiden Lane
11 York Road   Suite 704
London SE1 7NX   New York, NY 10038

www.continuumbooks.com

British Library Cataloguing-in-Publication Data
A catalogue record for this book is available from the British Library

ISBN: HB: 978–1–8470–6278–9
PB: 978–1–8470–6279–6

Library of Congress Cataloging-in-Publication Data
Delaney, James, 1977–
Starting with Rousseau / James Delaney.
p. cm.
Includes bibliographical references.
ISBN 978–1–84706–278–9—ISBN 978–1–84706–279–6
1. Rousseau, Jean-Jacques, 1712–1778.   I. Title.
B2137.D45 2009
194—dc22
2008053027

Typeset by RefineCatch Limited, Bungay, Suffolk
Printed and bound in Great Britain by
MPG Books Ltd, Bodmin, Cornwall

CONTENTS

CONTENTS

ACKNOWLEDGEMENTS

Jean-Jacques Rousseau has always been, for me, a philosopher to whom I felt a deep connection. In fact, it was in large part due to reading his *Discourse on the Origin of Inequality* that I decided to go into philosophy as a profession. I think this is because when I read his works, I genuinely felt that he was speaking directly to me, or at least to someone who grappled with the same questions, the same feelings of insecurity, and the same concerns that I did. And I almost always felt better about these things after reading him. In short, his works were, and continue to be, a source of comfort to me. Part of the reason that I was able to have such an experience was due to the wonderful professors I had during those undergraduate days. I therefore owe my thanks to two of those teachers in particular, E. Paul Colella, and Timothy Sean Quinn. Without their patient help and guidance, I may have never experienced the richness of Rousseau's thought or even philosophy in general. My hope is that this book might, in some way, do for new readers what my teachers did for me.

Trying to write a book on a figure like Rousseau is difficult in a number of ways. I wrestled with which texts to leave in, which to exclude, and how to put his ideas into a more contemporary context. I cannot say thank you enough to the many colleagues who helped me in this respect. One of these colleagues in particular deserves a special mention. Alexander U. Bertland helped in numerous ways to shape this book; by reading drafts of chapters, by pointing me toward texts of which I was previously unaware, and most of all by lending his own expertise on Rousseau. He offered his time and help with kindness and generosity, and I am extremely grateful to him.

To my friends and family, I thank you for your unwavering love and support while I undertook this project. My mother-in-law Arleen gave much of her own time so that I might have my own to write. This project simply could not have come to fruition without her help. I should also thank T. F. Greydensen for his unique help on this project. My wife Sarah helped me far too much and in far too many ways for me to ever put into words. To her I will simply say thank you for *everything*. And finally, I wish to dedicate this work to my son Jude.

CHAPTER 1

AN INTRODUCTION TO ROUSSEAU AND THE ENLIGHTENMENT PERIOD

i. THE ENLIGHTENMENT PERIOD

To understand Jean-Jacques Rousseau as a philosopher as well as a person, one must understand the time and place in which he lived. Typically Rousseau is referred to as an 'Enlightenment Thinker': the 'Enlightenment' was the term used to refer to a general attitude or project that was undertaken by several influential thinkers in the eighteenth century. Many of these names are still famous today and hold fairly significant places in the history of philosophy. French enlightenment thinkers who were contemporaries of Rousseau included Denis Diderot, D'Alembert, Baron de Montesquieu, Condillac and Voltaire. Perhaps the most important figure typically associated with the enlightenment is Immanuel Kant, on whom Rousseau would have a great influence.

It would be difficult, in only a few paragraphs, to summarize the enlightenment, but there are a few key themes to mention. Enlightenment thinkers shared a great sense of optimism about human reason. In the seventeenth and early eighteenth centuries, philosophers like John Locke and scientists like Sir Isaac Newton had made great progress in understanding the way the world works, how human knowledge is acquired, etc. They had done this in large part by breaking with traditional teachings that stretched back to medieval philosophy and indirectly all the way back to ancient Greek thought. At the core of the enlightenment project was the notion that the same kind of advances that were made in the areas of science and philosophy could similarly be made in social, moral and political life. However, a major influence on social, moral and political life at the time was the Church. It is therefore not surprising that many of the enlightenment thinkers viewed the Church with suspicion or even outright hostility. Voltaire in particular was outspoken in his criticism. The Church represented dogmatism and oppression to these thinkers; it represented clinging to an outdated and even superstitious set of principles that it saw fit to impose on the masses. One could classify the clash between the enlightenment and the Church as an intellectual struggle between classic traditional philosophy on one hand and progressive modern thinking on the other.

Rousseau's place in this struggle is not easily decided. He is often championed as one of the chief figures in the enlightenment, but his thought contrasts sharply from the themes discussed above in some very important ways. Some scholars have posed the question as: 'Rousseau: Classic or Modern?' On one hand, Rousseau's thought seems almost perfectly aligned with that of the enlightenment project. Rousseau was extremely sceptical of major organized religions, particularly those (like Christianity and specifically Roman Catholicism) that advocated a large amount of dogma. Rousseau, along with other enlightenment thinkers, was suspicious of this and in this sense was going against tradition. On a related matter, and perhaps even more importantly, Rousseau's political thought can be considered 'enlightenment'. He rejected the divine right of monarchs as well as the concept of 'natural inequality'. Instead, he argues vehemently that the only just sovereign to rule over a society is the collective will of the citizens themselves. In time, these political ideas were part of the inspiration for the French Revolution.

But Rousseau's thought also contains elements that run counter to the principles of the enlightenment. The very notions of progress and knowledge, which enlightenment thinkers like Voltaire championed, were condemned by Rousseau as a source of moral corruption. In the *Discourse on the Sciences and Arts*, Rousseau draws a parallel between intellectual progress and the decline of virtue. In the *Discourse on the Origin of Inequality*, he praises the noble savage, the concept of primitive pre-social human being, as being free of the vices that come from the implementation of 'civilized society'. Thus, Rousseau drew great criticism from his enlightenment contemporaries. And while he denounced many aspects of traditional organized religion, Rousseau was firm in his conviction that there was a God, supremely good and benevolent that intelligently directed the universe: an idea not generally shared by other enlightenment thinkers.

The result of Rousseau's strange identity as both a supporter of the enlightenment project as well as a critic of it is a large part of his philosophical legacy. For Rousseau personally, it left him feeling isolated and misunderstood. His friendships with his enlightenment thinkers all but dissolved, and the Church saw him and his ideas as a dangerous enemy. So, the question of whether Rousseau is 'classic or modern', or 'traditional or enlightenment', remains an open one. What is certain, however, is that Rousseau's ideas were and continue to be enormously important. They are thought provoking, controversial and at many times even beautiful. And they are more than just a historical curiosity. They have a timeless quality about them; his questions continue to be our questions, and his answers are often quite compelling.

ii. ROUSSEAU'S LIFE AND WORK

Rousseau was born in Geneva in 1712. His life began with trauma and heartbreak as his mother died from complications arising from his birth. His father, Isaac Rousseau, raised him during the early years of his childhood. Rousseau would later recall these early days with this father fondly. He speaks of reading great classical works, among them Plutarch. When he was still a young child, however, only about 10 years old, his father got into a dispute with a French captain. Fearing imprisonment over this dispute, Isaac Rousseau fled Geneva, and left his young son with relatives with whom he stayed until he later became an apprentice to an engraver. By Rousseau's own account, his apprenticeship was completely miserable and his master treated him more like a slave. So in 1728, after inadvertently being locked outside of Geneva's city gates after sundown, Rousseau simply fled. In his autobiography, the

Confessions, he talks of wandering about and staying with the kind people in the countryside who were willing to take him in.

It was around this time that Rousseau met Mme de Warens, a woman who would be a major influence on him through the early part of his life. She took him in and was instrumental in his religious conversion to Roman Catholicism. Geneva was a Protestant state, and so a result of this conversion was that Rousseau forfeited his citizenship. However, he never stopped associating himself proudly as a citizen of Geneva, and ultimately converted back to Protestantism and regained his citizenship in 1754. Throughout his writings, Rousseau always refers to Geneva as his 'fatherland' and paints it in an idealized sense.

Rousseau's first love was not philosophy, but music, and he even created a new system of musical notation that he presented in Paris to the Academy of Sciences in 1742. Though this ultimately proved unsuccessful, Rousseau did successfully write an opera, *The Village Soothsayer*, which was debuted in 1752 and was largely popular.

Shortly before this, Rousseau had become friendly with a group of French enlightenment thinkers known as the Encyclopaedists, who were given this name because of their collaboration of the grand, ambitious and now famous *Encyclopédie* project. The work was to be a kind of catalogue of human knowledge. The idea was conceived by Diderot, who co-edited the work with D'Alembert. Rousseau contributed several articles on music to the project. He also contributed an article on political economy that outlined the key themes of his political philosophy. At the heart of these enlightenment thinkers, as we saw in the section above, was both a sense that the advancement of reason would lead to the overall improvement of human society, and a negative attitude toward organized religion. Thus, Diderot was eventually imprisoned briefly for putting forth atheist views. While he was serving his sentence, Rousseau would often visit him, walking to and from the prison. On one of these walks, Rousseau had brought a book with him that announced an essay contest sponsored by the prestigious Academy of Dijon. The contest was to write an essay in response to the question of whether or not the progression of the sciences and arts had tended to purify morals. Inspired by the question, Rousseau set to work on an entry. The result was the *Discourse on the Sciences and Arts*, which won the Academy's contest prize in 1751. This work was an enormous success and made Rousseau a famous man of letters.

Several years before in 1744, Rousseau began a relationship with a woman named Thérèse Levasseur. Thérèse would become his lifelong partner though the two would not be officially married until 1768. The most noteworthy aspect of their relationship, and certainly the most notorious, is the fate of their five children, the first of which was born in 1746. Each of these children was given away to an orphanage, and Rousseau did not have a relationship with any of them. This, understandably, has led many to accuse Rousseau of being a hypocrite. After all, how can one reconcile the idea someone who stressed the importance of duty and of moral education with someone who simply abandoned five children. Rousseau speaks of this in his autobiography, and basically says with his typical self-loathing that these children were better off not knowing their father.

After the success of the *Discourse on the Sciences and Arts*, Rousseau continued writing philosophy as well as music. His next major philosophical work was once again a response to an essay contest from the Academy of Dijon. This time, the question concerned the source and legitimacy of the inequality among men. Rousseau's answer, *The Discourse on the Origin of Inequality Among Men* did not win the Academy's prize, but it is generally regarded as a superior philosophical piece when compared to his *First Discourse*. It was also around this time that his relationship with the Encyclopaedists began to deteriorate. To a large extent this began when D'Alembert wrote an entry on Geneva in the *Encyclopédie*, in which he suggested the Genevans might benefit from establishing a public theatre. Rousseau's response was his famous 1758 *Letter to D'Alembert*, in which he railed against the theatre and the vices he believes it would bring to Geneva. After this he had a bitter falling out with Diderot, D'Alembert and Grimm, and even suspected them of trying to sabotage him personally and professionally.

During the late 1750s, Rousseau was working on two very ambitious projects that would help in large part to shape his philosophical legacy. One, the *Emile*, was a work on the philosophy of education, which attempted to show how to raise a morally virtuous human being and citizen. The work also had a sustained account of Rousseau's so-called 'religion of nature' which ran contrary to Catholic Church teaching. The second work, *The Social Contract*, was Rousseau's most comprehensive work of political philosophy. In it, Rousseau outlines the features that would make for an ideal state, stressing the importance of unity, equality and the duty of citizens. Both *Emile* and *The Social Contract* were published in 1762. Rousseau, by all accounts, was quite proud of these works and thought them a contribution not only to academic circles, but to the whole of society. It therefore came as quite a shock to him that both, especially because of the religious views expressed in *Emile*, were immediately banned by Parisian authorities and his arrest was ordered. What was even more heartbreaking to him, however, was that these works were condemned and burned in Geneva as well. Rousseau suspected Geneva was bowing to pressure from the French to do this, but nevertheless, he renounced his Genevan citizenship in 1763. He fled Paris, settling briefly with David Hume, until a quarrel ended his stay.

Rousseau continued writing during this unhappy period, publishing his *Dictionary on Music* in 1763 as well as his *Letter to Beaumont*, an attempt to justify the religious views he advocated in *Emile*. He also started working on his autobiography, the *Confessions*, which would be published posthumously. Eventually in 1770, he moved back to Paris where he copied music for a living and gave public readings from his *Confessions*. He also began writing two additional autobiographical works, the *Dialogues: Rousseau, Judge of Jean-Jacques* and the *Reveries of the Solitary Walker*, both of which were also published after his death. In his latter years, Rousseau became more and more convinced that there was a grand conspiracy against him, and in many ways his autobiographical works are an attempt to defend himself against it. Most believe that at least some or even most of this was a result of Rousseau's own paranoia. In 1778, Rousseau died at the age of 66.

iii. THE STRUCTURE OF THIS BOOK

This book, in keeping with the 'Starting With' series, is intended first and foremost as an aid to those approaching Jean-Jacques Rousseau's writings for the first time. I have tried to write it in such a way that it will speak to the contemporary reader, but have made every attempt not to distort what I take to be Rousseau's intended meaning in the works I discuss and the passages I quote. As a general rule for studying any historically significant philosopher, I believe there is a danger if one depends too much on secondary literature. Many of these philosophers, partly because of their writing style and partly because of the complexity of the ideas they are trying to address, can be very challenging. But, there is really no substitute for reading the primary sources themselves. No matter how much an author tries to be impartial and objective in summarizing someone else's thought, it will always, in some sense, be an interpretation once removed from the original. This book is no exception, and so I would urge readers to use it as a supplement and not a substitute to reading Rousseau's own words. Perhaps unlike some historical thinkers, I think this is particularly important when it comes to Rousseau. For an important part of understanding him, of *really* understanding him, is not only comprehending the claims he makes but seeing the way in which those claims are made. Rousseau writes with a style, eloquence and passion that is truly unique among philosophers. Though his meaning can sometimes be difficult to discern, this passion comes though. For me, and I think for most Rousseau scholars, this is part of what initially draws us to him. Reading Rousseau can really be a pleasure, so I urge those reading this book not to deprive themselves of it.

Critics of Rousseau, both among his contemporaries and among present day commentators, often accuse his work as lacking uniformity. The words used to describe this problem are 'paradoxical', 'contradictory' and 'hypocritical'. Some of these critics suggest that Rousseau's works are therefore best read in isolation from one another. His political philosophy in *The Social Contract* it is sometimes said, for example, cannot be connected philosophically with themes of his novel like *Julie* or the narrative account in *Emile*.

Though, as I said above, I have tried to remain impartial in my presentation of Rousseau, I nevertheless favour a different view that this book no doubt reflects. I think that there are fundamental themes in Rousseau's philosophy, among them the natural goodness of uncorrupted human beings, the notion of a moral order and intelligence that directs the universe and the idea of virtue and fulfilment resting in regarding oneself with a healthy self-love independent of arbitrary social expectations. Most Rousseau scholars, I think, would agree with these general claims. But, I think that there are rich connections to be made between Rousseau's works that can better illustrate them. In my view, these connections help to elucidate, rather than muddle, Rousseau's philosophy as whole.

For this reason I have tried to point the reader to parallels between the different works I discuss. The reader will notice that I will often say things like 'this theme will be discussed further in the following chapter' or 'as we saw in earlier discussions in previous chapters'. But I have tried to do this without sacrificing the ability of the reader to go directly to certain chapters of interest without having to carefully read the chapters preceding it. Thus, if one is particularly interested in forming an understanding of the *Discourse on the Origin of Inequality*, I believe the third chapter can stand alone as a useful tool in this respect. My hope is that each of the chapters themselves, as well as the sub-sections in chapters dealing with multiple works, can stand alone in this way.

CHAPTER 2

PROGRESS AND MODERN SOCIETY

i. INTRODUCTION

'Progress' is a term that we use often in everyday language. We can talk about the progress we make as individuals in various endeavours like education or athletics; for example 'so and so has made great progress: in his math skills'. We can also talk about collective progress that which involves groups or whole societies over time. We might say that over the past 100 years medicine has made great progress. Both as individuals and as societies, progress is associated with improvement; progress is a good thing. In many ways, modernity is tied to the notion of progress, as making progress is in large part what we think distinguishes our modern age from past ages. And during Rousseau's time, the Enlightenment, progress was championed.

What about 'moral progress'? It cannot really be doubted that we have made progress in areas of knowledge like science. But, as a society and as individuals, are we really *better people*? To some extent we take it for granted that we are morally better, or at least that we have learned important moral lessons from mistakes in the past that we are determined not to repeat ourselves. But Rousseau challenges this assumption. The three works discussed in this chapter, the *Discourse on the Sciences and Arts*, the *Letter to D'Alembert* and *Julie or the New Heloise* are all, I believe, important in the sense that they contribute to this challenge in important ways. For in each of them, there is a degree of caution about modern progress, one that warns against the danger of true virtue being replaced by false images or mere appearances.

In the *Discourse on the Sciences and Arts*, which was Rousseau's first major philosophical piece, the false image of virtue is an arbitrary set of manners and etiquette brought about by our preoccupations with the progress of the sciences and arts. In the *Letter to D'Alembert*, Rousseau attacks the idea of establishing a theatre in his homeland of Geneva. D'Almebert, one of the editors and major contributors of the *Encyclopédie* (a major accomplishment of the Enlightenment) suggested a theatre might improve the already exemplary morality there. But, according to Rousseau, theatre too would be a distraction from virtue and would actually bring vices. And finally, in Rousseau's novel *Julie*, the characters live in the purity of the countryside, away from the corrupting influence of large 'modern' cities. There are of course other themes to these works, and any one of them could warrant a discussion in its own right. Nevertheless, I think beginning with them is a good way to familiarize oneself with Rousseau's style, and some of the more basic aspects of his thought.

ii. THE DISCOURSE ON THE SCIENCES AND ARTS

The *Discourse on the Sciences and Arts*, or '*First Discourse*', is the work that originally gained Rousseau fame and recognition. Published in 1750, it was a response to an essay contest put forth by the Academy of Dijon on the following question: 'Has the restoration of the sciences and arts tended to purify morals?' In other words, as technological advances were made and culture enriched, have people themselves become better? I think most people, even today, are at first inclined to say that the answer to this question is yes. We think we are making moral progress along with our progress in the sciences and arts. Good evidence for this is how quick we are to look at troubling historical events (slavery, for example) and think to ourselves that now, given our progress, we would never make such mistakes again. People in the past, we like to think, did not have our superior moral perspective. Certainly in Rousseau's time, the age of the enlightenment, these attitudes prevailed as well.

Recall the discussion of the enlightenment in the previous chapter. So it is somewhat ironic and a bit surprising that Rousseau's essay, the entry that ultimately won the Academy's prize, answered the question of whether the restoration of the sciences and arts has tended to purify morals with a resounding 'No'.

This irony was certainly not lost on Rousseau and in his brief introduction to the *First Discourse* he admits as much when he says, 'How can one dare blame the sciences before one of Europe's most learned Societies, praise ignorance in a famous Academy and reconcile contempt of study with respect for the truly learned?'[1] Having seen these 'apparent contradictions' Rousseau defends himself by saying that he is not attacking science, but rather defending virtue. Although it is subtle, this point is crucial for understanding the *First Discourse*. Rousseau's central criticism is *not* that the sciences and arts are in themselves intrinsically bad. Rather, they are not intrinsically good either; their advance does not necessarily coincide with moral progress. It does seem fair to say, however that the sciences and arts may have intrinsic dangers that come with them. Therefore, it is quite possible (and indeed this is exactly what Rousseau thinks has actually happened) that focusing on the advance of the sciences and arts can come at the expense of moral progress. To put it simply, we spend so much time on them that we forget to worry about being virtuous. Morality becomes neglected.

A relatively short text, the *First Discourse* consists of two parts, simply entitled the 'First Part' and the 'Second Part.' Preceding them is a preface and brief introduction, part of which I quoted above. The substance of the preface, like the introduction, is primarily a chance for Rousseau to prepare the readers for what he thinks will be his unpopular response to the Academy's question. The First Part works largely by examining history. Rousseau attempts to show that past societies that emphasized the sciences and arts were less virtuous than those who did not. The Second Part examines the 'sciences and arts in themselves'; in it, Rousseau articulates the dangers that come with their practice, as well as what their proper place should be in a society. I have put the majority of my discussion of the *First Discourse* into two sections corresponding to these First and Second Parts.

First Part

The First Part opens with what Rousseau sees as an important distinction between what we might call 'true virtue' on one hand, and what is typically referred to as virtue in societies consumed by advances of the sciences and arts on the other. Far from advocating true virtue, these societies praise superficial customs that are essentially nothing more than etiquette. Among members of these societies, Rousseau argues, we praise those who are well-dressed or 'cultured' rather than those who are truly good like farmers. Farmers may not have fancy clothes or knowledge of the 'finer things in life', but what they do have is far more important. They are strong, independent, and are unconcerned with superficial things like social status which are ultimately unimportant. In a word, they are much closer to nature. One should note that this theme, associating virtue with nature, is one of the most important in all of Rousseau's thought. In future chapters we shall see it played out, albeit in different manifestations, in major works such as the *Discourse on the Origin of Inequality*, the *Emile*, the *Social Contract*. Indeed, most of our vices, Rousseau argues, come about from having our pure human nature corrupted. The sciences and arts have done this by making us replace virtue with social etiquette:

> Before art had moulded our manners and taught our passions to speak an affected language, our customs were rustic but natural, and differences of conduct announced at first glance those of character. Human nature, basically, was no better, but men found their security in the ease of seeing through each other, and that advantage, which we no longer appreciate, spared them a great many vices.[2]

Here, we see Rousseau arguing that another problem follows from allowing these social customs to assume the place of virtue in society. They allow, or perhaps even force, people to hide their true selves. This is what Rousseau means in the above quote when he says that in societies in which this corruption has not taken place, people 'found their security in the ease of seeing through each other'. But, what does he mean by this? If we read further, I think the message is clear.

As I read him, Rousseau is warning against two effects. The first is that we will become so obsessed with acting according to these social customs that in our own minds we will actually substitute them for true virtue. Hence he says there will be, 'No more sincere friendships; no real esteem, no more well-based confidence. Suspicions, offenses, fears, coldness, reserve, hate, betrayal will hide constantly under that uniform and false veil of politeness'.[3] Though it may not be a perfect analogy to what Rousseau is getting at, we might consider the current day criticism that many make of our own society that we have become 'overly politically correct'. Now I should caution that I do not use this example because I think that political correctness in all its form is a bad thing; far from it. Clearly there are offensive and hurtful words that we should not use. However, it has become something of a joke in recent years that we have a politically correct term for everything, and the fact that we become horribly offended when someone uses a politically incorrect term can in some cases show how far we have really gotten away from what is really important in such matters. Imagine that someone uses the wrong term to refer to some group, but only because he was not sure what the politically correct term was, and he had no animosity whatsoever toward the group in question. But imagine that the person is immediately labelled as insensitive, prejudiced or bigoted. I think Rousseau would look at this as an unfortunate case in which the politeness of agreed upon 'right' words for things replaced virtue. And we could certainly imagine opposite cases in which someone was always very careful to speak in politically correct language, but actually held insensitive, prejudiced or bigoted views. This, then, is one general worry Rousseau has.

The second dangerous effect that can come from replacing virtue with social custom, which Rousseau says can come from advancing the sciences and arts, is a kind of apathy: 'National hatreds will die out, but so will love of country. For scorned ignorance, a dangerous Pyrrhonism will be substituted'.[4] Since there is no true virtue, but rather only an arbitrary collection of politeness, people will become increasingly sceptical and cynical. They will lack any real sense of pride in their society, or of seeing themselves as part of a larger whole, which as we shall see in Chapter 5 is a major theme of Rousseau's political philosophy.

But Rousseau thinks that these ills, which he is observing in his own society, are by no means a new phenomenon. For one need only look to history to see that in the vast majority of societies, virtue has been neglected in proportion to the degree to which the arts and sciences were advanced. As evidence for this claim, Rousseau mentions several past societies as well as some contemporary examples. Egypt, he argues, was the dominant power in the world before it became the 'mother of philosophy'. Soon after, it was conquered by the Cambyses, then the Greeks, the Romans, the Arabs and the Turks. Greece, too, was once strong and its people virtuous. But like Egypt, it also became corrupted when the sciences and arts advanced. With Rome and Constantinople, the story is the same. The latter, the so-called refuge of the arts and sciences, Rousseau describes as 'all that is most shameful in debauchery and corruption, most heinous in betrayals, assassinations and poisons, most atrocious in the combination of all crimes'.[5] Finally, Rousseau cites China as a current day example of a society who bestows the highest honours and power upon those who advance the sciences, but argues that there is no vice which does not dominate them.

History, however, does give us positive examples of societies that focused on virtue rather than the sciences and arts. Among these are the first Persians, the Scythians and the ancient German tribes. What is more is that these societies neglected the advancement of the sciences intentionally. They were fully aware, Rousseau argues, that in other lands people were pursuing such things, but recognized that such pursuits were vain and threatened their morals.

The society that Rousseau praises the most, however, is Sparta. He contrasts it with Athens, which he sees as yet another example of a society rich in culture, arts, science, knowledge and philosophy, but whose morals were completely corrupt. This might strike one as a bit ironic. Rousseau, a philosopher himself, is criticizing the city that is generally associated with the birth of western philosophy: the city of Socrates, Plato and Aristotle. But in terms of the rustic and natural virtue Rousseau is praising in the *First Discourse*, it is not surprising that he would prefer Sparta to Athens. In fact, as we shall see in subsequent chapters, Sparta is mentioned positively in many of Rousseau's other major works as well. Among these are the *Emile* and *Social Contract*. Whether or not Rousseau is painting a historically accurate picture of these two ancient Greek city-states is certainly questionable. Certainly Sparta was not perfect, though one might think it was, based on Rousseau's description. In the following chapter we shall see a similar issue in Rousseau's description of his homeland of Geneva in the dedication to the *Discourse on the Origin of Inequality*.

Historical accuracy aside, Rousseau's Sparta holds those key characteristics the First Part has articulated as necessary for virtue to flourish:

> Oh Sparta! You eternally put to shame a vain doctrine! While the vices which accompany the fine arts entered Athens together with them, while a tyrant there so carefully collected the works of the prince of poets, you chased the arts and artists, the sciences and scientists away from your walls.[6]

If Athens is corrupt, and Sparta virtuous, one might rightly ask how Rousseau views those incredibly influential Athenian thinkers mentioned above. For one of them at least, Socrates, he offers some thoughts. Socrates, according to Rousseau, was indeed a wise man, but he went against the vain culture of Athens; this ultimately led to his execution. If we look at the Plato's account of Socrates in the *Apology*, we see the now famous account of Socratic knowledge consisting in simply knowing that one does not know. Those whom Socrates criticizes, poets, statesmen, artists, etc. are not wise precisely because they think they are experts on truth and virtue, but they actually know nothing. This kind of arrogance leads to exactly the kind of corruption of morals Rousseau is concerned with, and it comes with the advancement of the sciences and arts. Socrates is praised in large part because unlike the poets, statesmen and artists, he is truly honest.

Second Part

In the Second Part of the *First Discourse*, as we have already said, Rousseau attempts to examine the sciences and arts 'in themselves'. And while he does do this in large part, the implications that he draws impact several other important aspects of social life. Among these are luxury, military strength and education. All of these, Rousseau will argue, are negatively impacted by, or negative results of, the advancement of the sciences and arts.

The Second Part opens by drawing a parallel between the pursuit of science and vanity. In fact, Rousseau argues that the sciences 'arise in vanity'. This claim is certainly at odds with the general theme of the Enlightenment, which saw the cultivation of reason and the understanding of the world as a kind of liberating way to escape the superstition and ignorance which had plagued human beings throughout history. Rousseau's claim is at odds with classical authors as well, perhaps most notably Plato and Aristotle. It was Aristotle who identified 'pure contemplation of the highest things' to be the most pleasant and noble activity that humans are capable of performing.[7] Why does Rousseau think that such intellectual pursuits are harmful? Primarily, it is because he does not believe that they have any real practical import. Contemplating the deep eternal questions of philosophy and science, for him, does not ultimately lead one to act any differently in his or her daily life. Furthermore, Rousseau believes that those who pursue these questions are well aware that they lack this practical significance. We pursue these questions, Rousseau argues, not because of any noble intellectual curiosity, but rather out of simple vanity:

> In fact, whether one leafs through the annals of the world or supplements uncertain chronicles with philosophic research, human learning will not be found to have an origin corresponding to the idea we like to have of it. Astronomy was born from superstition; eloquence from ambition, hate, flattery and falsehood; geometry from avarice; physics from curiosity; all, even moral philosophy, from human pride. Thus the sciences and

arts owe their birth to our vices; we would be less doubtful of their advantages if they owed it to our virtues.[8]

If one doubts that the sciences have any practical application, Rousseau considers some of the 'advances' they have made. Some of these include matters of physics like the proportions that govern the attraction of bodies in a vacuum; philosophical arguments such as how the mind and body could interact with one another and biological observations such as the breeding patterns of insects. He then asks whether any of these 'advances' has really served to make our lives better. The answer, Rousseau thinks, is clearly no.

The 'vices' Rousseau describes here require something else before the sciences can be pursued, namely 'idleness'. Since the sciences lack any real practical application, it makes sense to think that they can only be pursued when one has her immediate and most basic needs satisfied. Hence, the sciences are 'born in idleness'. However, to continue their pursuit, one needs even more idle time to spend. So science actually perpetuates idleness and takes people away from what is really important, namely their practical, moral and civil duties.

Finally, and perhaps worst of all, the sciences do more than ignore the practical that is true virtue. They actually have a negative effect on virtue: 'They [philosophers] smile disdainfully at the old-fashioned words of fatherland and religion, and devote their talents and philosophy to debasing all that is sacred among men.'[9] Philosophers give confusing paradoxes, and overly confuse things, especially the principles of basic 'common sense morality'. The vice of idleness initially makes possible, and then is sustained by, the pursuit of the sciences.

In addition to idleness, the 'evil of wasting time', there is a second evil that Rousseau says often accompanies the pursuit of the sciences and arts, namely 'Luxury'. He argues that luxury rarely develops with them. Luxury is dangerous because it is yet another distraction from virtue for citizens; societies that are immersed in luxury are consumed by wealth. This leads to the valuing of everything in terms of money. Thus, Rousseau tells us that ancient societies talked of morals and virtue, but the politicians of his day talk only of business. We might notice a similar phenomenon in our own society. How often do we settle seemingly moral disputes by simply doing a cost benefit analysis rather than really asking what is the right thing to do. The discussion of idleness we have just described focused to a great degree on the sciences (philosophy, physics, biology, etc.), but Rousseau's criticism of luxury leads him more directly to a discussion of the arts.

Every artist, Rousseau says, wants to be praised. Therefore, artists are somewhat trapped by opinions of the societies in which they live. If the society is consumed with frivolous things rather than virtue and true beauty, artists will produce works that appeal to those frivolous things. A great artist will 'lower his genius to the level of his time, and will prefer to compose ordinary works which are admired during his lifetime instead of marvels which would not be admired until long after his death'.[10] The ordinary works are the effect of the public's bad taste; the artists are simply giving the public what they want. However, this only perpetuates the society's bad taste. And if an artist refuses to conform to society's frivolous vision of what art should be, she will die in poverty and disgrace.

I think it is worth pausing for a moment as Rousseau's discussion does not seem to be so much an indictment of art, but rather luxury. He seems to be saying that the quality of art is simply determined by the degree to which a society values luxury. A high priority on luxury will result in art of a low quality, whereas a society that is not consumed with luxury will produce art of a high quality. If this is the case, it seems that the *First Discourse* is really about the sciences and *luxury*, not the sciences and *arts*. This ambiguity is a bit difficult to reconcile, but I think it can best be understood as follows. What we typically think of as 'art' in a depraved society is in fact nothing more than a reflection of our emphasis on superficial luxuries. Thus, when Rousseau is attacking art, I think it is this mistaken notion or 'false image' that he has in mind, and certainly it inhibits, rather than contributes to, moral progress.

Cultivating the sciences and arts is also harmful to a society's specifically military virtue, and this too corresponds to the spread of luxury. For it also has the effect of damaging true courage. Rousseau's support for this claim rests once again on historical induction. In one particularly interesting example, he mentions that when they ravaged Greece, the Goths did not burn the libraries. The reason for this was the Goths thought it better that they allow their enemies to keep their books since they would turn them away from military exercise. This and other examples, Rousseau tells us, 'teach us that in such military regulations, and in all regulations that resemble them, study of the sciences is much more apt to soften and enervate courage than to strengthen and animate it'.[11] I think that we can draw from Rousseau's earlier discussion of the sciences as lacking any practical application to see why he makes this claim. After all, if contemplating the soul's relationship to the body and the breeding habits of insects cannot help us to take pride in our ordinary lives as citizens, it is even more difficult to see how they would be of any help in making someone into a good soldier. The arts too have a damaging effect on the military. Rousseau claims that by the Romans' own admission, their military virtue died proportionately to the degree to which they 'became connoisseurs of paintings, engravings, jewelled vessels, and began to cultivate the fine arts'.[12] To use a current day expression, Rousseau's argument about the dangers of arts and sciences with respect to military virtue is that they 'make us soft'. Being cultured, philosophical and civilized does not help one to be brave, rugged and courageous.

Even more damaging than the effect the sciences and arts have on military virtue, however, is the effect they have on education. Education, in the broad sense of teaching someone from an early age how to be 'good', is an idea in which Rousseau had a great interest. In fact, one of his most important and comprehensive works, *Emile*, is dedicated to it. The fourth chapter of this book is dedicated to it.

Not surprisingly, when Rousseau looks at the education of young people in his own society, one that ignores virtue, he sees children learning everything except their duties. They learn languages that they will never need to speak, they learn obscure historical facts, but they never really learn how to think for themselves. Furthermore, they do this to *appear* wise and virtuous. And more importantly, they do not learn to love their country and their fellow citizens. Following these claims about education, Rousseau moves to a more general description of society's misplaced priorities and offers something in the way of an explanation for precisely why the emphasis on the sciences and arts has the negative effect he has been describing:

> What brings about all these abuses if not the disastrous inequality introduced among men by the distinction of talents and the debasement of virtues? That is the most evident effect of all our studies and the most dangerous of all their consequences. One no longer asks if a man is upright, bur rather if he is talented; nor of a book if it is useful, but if it is well written. Rewards are showered on the witty, and virtue is left without honors.[13]

These themes, namely proper moral education, pride in one's citizenship and the dangers produced by inequality, are left some somewhat unclear and ambiguous in *First Discourse*. But they are some of the most important in Rousseau's thought. We shall see him argue fervently for them and in much more detail in the coming chapters when we consider his other major works, especially *Discourse on the Origin of Inequality*, *Emile*, and *Social Contract*.

Before concluding our discussion on *First Discourse*, I should say something about its curious and somewhat ironic ending. For at this point, one might rightly ask 'should anyone ever try to engage in the sciences and arts?' It would seem that the risks are simply too great, as the threat to virtue should make them off limits so to speak. But Rousseau does not go quite this far. Instead, he says that nature has bestowed upon a very few an almost innate ability to pursue knowledge. He mentions a few such people by name, Francis Bacon, Descartes and Newton. So advanced are they that they do not even need teachers; in fact, teachers would only hinder them. He states:

> If a few men must be allowed to devote themselves to the study of the sciences and arts, in must be only those who feel the strength to walk alone in their footsteps and go beyond them. It is for these few to raise monuments to the glory of human intellect.[14]

With the exception of these few, the rest of us (and Rousseau includes himself here rather than with the very few gifted) should try to live simple lives dedicated to virtue. Ultimately this life will be more pleasant for us anyway; for we will not be striving always for the approval of others, and putting our own sense of self-worth in whether or not others think we are talented, cultured, smart or artistic. And so ends the *First Discourse*.

iii. LETTER TO D'ALEMBERT

The letter to D'Alembert is, among other things, a continuation of some of the criticisms of the arts initially put forth by Rousseau in the *First Discourse*. D'Alembert, as mentioned in the introduction to this chapter, was a co-editor a major contributor to the *Encyclopédie*. In 1758, in its seventh volume, D'Alembert wrote an entry on Geneva, Rousseau's birth place. Though it forms only a relatively small part of the entry itself, D'Alembert recommends that Geneva have a public theatre. Rousseau then wrote the letter as an objection to this recommendation. Since I have limited space, it is not possible to look at all of Rousseau's arguments in the letter. However, I believe I can outline D'Alembert's recommendation as well as the more critical aspects of Rousseau's reply.

D'Alembert's discussion of Geneva in the *Encyclopédie* is overwhelmingly positive; he explains that drama is forbidden in Geneva because its citizens fear the corruption of morals that would come from having the actors within its walls. The fear, he says, is that with the actors would come a taste for adornment, dissipation and libertinism, and these will be especially damaging to the youth. However, D'Alembert is optimistic that these dangers could be avoided. He suggests that the Genevans could enforce strict laws that would control the conduct of the actors. If they did this, Geneva could avoid the corruption of their morals, while enjoying all of the moral benefits that the theatre brings. He describes these benefits as follows:

> ... the theatrical performances would form the taste of the citizens and would give them the fineness of tact, a delicacy of

sentiments, which is very difficult to acquire without the help of theatrical performances; literature would profit without the process of libertinism, and Geneva would join to the prudence of Lacedaemon the urbanity of Athens.[15]

According to D'Alembert, the theatre's negative effects could be sufficiently controlled with laws, and its positive effects on culture and morality would be most valuable to Geneva. These are the central claims Rousseau challenges.

Rousseau's letter to D'Alembert is a fairly lengthy document, longer in fact than the *First Discourse*. Aside from some preliminary remarks in which Rousseau criticizes aspects D'Alembert's characterization of Geneva's religious ministers, the whole of the work argues against the institution of a public theatre. Some of these objections can be considered criticisms of theatre *per se*, while others speak to problems specifically associated with a theatre in Geneva. Generally speaking, Rousseau's arguments can be divided into two types: those that counter the claim that theatre actually brings benefits to society, and those that argue that particular negative effects will either necessarily, or very likely, result from theatre. To support his arguments, Rousseau discusses many different examples of plays that he thinks are either wrongly thought to produce societal benefits, or which he thinks have harmful effects.

Rousseau says that the question 'Is the Theater good or bad in itself?' is too vague, because theatre can only be judged by its effects on a people. It seems, therefore, that we could say that a theatre that actually did have good effects on the people would then be good. So perhaps Rousseau is agnostic about the theatre's intrinsic value, or at the very least, he thinks it is value neutral. In this way, his discussion of it is very similar to his discussion of the arts in the Second Part of the *First Discourse*. Just as art can perpetuate the bad traits of a public with a corrupted morality, and Rousseau tells us the following about theatre:

> The Stage is, in general, a painting of the human passions, the original of which is in every heart. But if the Painter neglected to flatter these passions, the Spectators would soon be repelled and

would not want to see themselves in a light which made them despise themselves. So that, if he gives an odious coloring to some passions, it is only to those that are not general and naturally hated. Hence, the Author, in this respect, only follows public sentiment.[16]

We can understand this passage, and the argument it supports, as a criticism of one of the supposed major benefits of the theatre. D'Alembert himself advocated it; namely, the theatre can tell stories of great virtue that will help shape the real virtue of those who watch it. But, Rousseau is telling us that theatre is incapable of really shaping people in this way. Their moral characters are already shaped and are reflected in public opinion. So we are really left with four possibilities: a virtuous public watching a play that reflects vice, which would serve no good; a corrupted public watching a play that reflects vice, which also would serve no good; a virtuous public watching a play that reflects vice, which would disinterest or repulse them, but would not serve a good that is would not make them any better morally. Finally, and most importantly, there is the possibility of a corrupted public watching a play that reflects virtue. But the public's opinion, corrupted as it is, will not be moved by the play at all. They too will be either repulsed by it, or simply ignore it.

Rousseau began this discussion by telling us that the theatre can only be said to be good or bad with respect to its effects on the people; but he is now telling us that with respect to forming the moral character of its audience members, the theatre can *have no effect*. This is because, according to Rousseau, theatre can only really move us at the level of emotion. All of the emotions, or passions as he also calls them, are 'sisters' that is, they are always aroused together. Passions are insufficient for really changing our moral outlook. Only reason can do that, and reason, Rousseau claims, has no effect on the theatre. Thus, the most powerful argument for the benefits of the theatre, which is that it serves to cultivate and increase public virtue, fails.

If the theatre will not bring benefits, the next question is what harms it might bring. Rousseau thinks there are several. One harm he thinks will be a negative impact on society's view of women. Women, by nature, have the power of resistance. We shall see in future chapters, especially in our discussions of the *Second Discourse* and the *Emile* that Rousseau feels strongly about this. The 'power of resistance' actually makes women the stronger sex in Rousseau's eyes. Men, by nature, are stronger physically. But, ultimately women have the ability to control men when it comes to romantic relationships. To put it simply, men are enchanted by women, fascinated with them. This power, when exercised properly, amounts to feminine virtue for Rousseau. But when corrupted, like all faculties, it becomes a vice. The theatre leads to this corruption primarily because it takes this level of fascination too far. The theatre portrays women as too perfect, as all-knowing and superior. This ultimately does real women a disservice and results in a distorted view of them.

A second harm is that the theatre will increase bad taste and an emphasis on luxury (again we should recall Rousseau's criticisms in the *First Discourse* on this subject). In large cities, of which Rousseau is generally sceptical to begin with (we shall see this more in the *Emile*), theatres will only enhance the vice, idleness and mischievousness that is already there. But his caution is even stronger when it comes to theatres in small cities, which is presumably closer to the way he envisions Geneva. To show this, Rousseau gives us an interesting thought experiment. He tells us of a small city in the mountains he once visited in his youth. The people there were happy farmers who worked hard and entertained each other with their own company and fellowship. They would also spend their time working on crafts such as woodworking and watch making. They would keep some of the products of these crafts, and sell some to foreigners. They also had interests in music, sketching and painting. All in all, they had a rather blissful and happy existence. Now what would happen, Rousseau asks, if this small city built a public theatre? If the people gain a taste for it, they will begin to abandon their labour and other amusements in favour of the theatre. The cost of going, no matter how small, will begin to emphasize inequalities in wealth. Additionally, the efforts the people will make in dressing up to go to the performances will perpetuate the new emphasis on wealth. In the winter, public funds will be needed to ensure the roads are clear so people will be able to go, which will once again increase inequalities of wealth. All this will lead to citizens being concerned with appearances and luxury, and will be at the expense of virtue, which was quite strong before the theatre was built.

Another harm speaks in direct response to one mentioned by D'Alembert, namely the corrupting influence of actors. Recall that D'Alembert thought that strict laws could protect against this negative influence. Rousseau is far less optimistic about this. Actors, he claims, are given to disorder and actresses are given to scandal. His evidence for this is largely empirical. He argues that it can be observed everywhere that actors are either viewed with suspicion or in some cases viewed as horrifying altogether. He is therefore sceptical that 'strict laws' could keep them in line. But Rousseau thinks there is an even more fundamental problem with actors; one that is intrinsically tied to the profession itself:

> What is the talent of the actor? It is in the art of counterfeiting himself, or putting on another character than his own, of appearing different than he is, of becoming passionate in cold blood, of saying what he does not think as naturally as if he really did think it, and, finally, of forgetting his own place by dint of taking another's. What is the profession of the actor? It is a trade in which he performs for money, submits himself, to the disgrace and the affronts that other buy the right to give him, and puts him publically on sale. I beg every sincere man to tell if he does not feel in the depths of his soul that there is something servile and base in this traffic of oneself.[17]

This criticism might strike us as a bit strange. We typically do not think that acting is somehow intrinsically tied to some sort of moral corruption. But it is perhaps not surprising that Rousseau would take this view. The arguments in the *Letter to D'Alembert* as well as those we have observed above in the *First Discourse* have at least one general theme in common: a society is harmed when false images replace virtue. The actor, when he acts, is putting on a false image, namely the character he is playing. Rousseau is therefore suspicious because the very act itself seems analogous to a corrupt society.

The preceding has in large part been a discussion of arguments against the theatre in general. But before concluding, we should note some of Rousseau's objections to a theatre specifically in Geneva. First, he raises a purely practical problem of sustainability. He argues that Geneva, primarily because of its size and partly because of the make up of its citizenry, would not support a theatre. However, even if those difficulties were surmounted, and a theatre was established there would be a very detrimental effect.

In Geneva, there were social groups formed by the people in which they would dine, drink, gamble and go on outings. Typically these groups of about 15 or so people met in taverns and were referred to simply as *circles*. One of Rousseau's biggest fears about a public theatre in Geneva is that it would result in the loss of these social groups. If the theatre was successful, it would become the social outlet instead of the *circles*. We have already seen what Rousseau says will be the resulting effect or lack thereof of theatre on morals. By contrast, the *circles* serve a valuable purpose, establishing a healthy interaction of men, as well as true fraternity, friendship and genuine love of fatherland. In addition to the *circles*, Rousseau also advocates grand festivals as a means of social interaction. These too, he argues, would suffer should a theatre be built?

An argument against theatre undoubtedly strikes most contemporary readers as outrageous, and likely a blatant violation of free speech rights. But I believe the *Letter to D'Alembert*, while probably not convincing as an argument for us to abolish the theatre altogether (and in our case movies, television, etc.), can perhaps at least raise our critical awareness of these media. Do the shows and movies we watch make us any better morally? Do they ever corrupt us? Do they ever distract us from our moral and civil duties? If we answer yes, then perhaps there is something to what Rousseau is saying in this letter. The solution of a ban is likely too extreme a measure to take in remedying such problems. However, being aware of these issues, and thinking of *some* ways of minimizing their harms is an exercise in which we probably should be engaged on some level.

iv. JULIE OR THE NEW HELOISE

Published in 1761, *Julie or the New Heloise* is a novel, one that was extremely successful and widely read. Because it is a work of fiction, it is a different kind of book than Rousseau's more straightforwardly philosophical pieces. The philosophical works, discussions of which form the vast majority of this book, contain claims and arguments that I am trying to convey to the reader. Thus, as a novel, *Julie* does not lend itself to that kind of discussion. However, I think it is appropriate to include a short discussion of it here, in the hope that I can articulate some of the philosophical themes it has in common with the philosophical writings.

There is some historical controversy surrounding the title of the book. Typically, the entire title is expressed as follows: *Julie or the New Heloise: Letters of Two Lovers Who Live in a Small Town at the Foot of the Alps*. In some of the editions that followed the book's initial publication, as well as the great amount of secondary literature written about it, the novel is referred to by some simply as *Julie*, and by others as the *New Heloise*. The name 'Heloise' holds particular historical significance. In the twelfth century, the famous medieval philosopher Pierre Abelard tutored and fell in love with his pupil Heloise. They had a child and secretly married, but when her guardian found out their secret, he had Abelard castrated. This story was well known during Rousseau's time after their letters were published. So Rousseau is drawing on this tragic love story for his own novel. But mainly for the sake of brevity, I will refer to it here simply as *Julie*. As the full title suggests, however, it is written in the form of letters, most of them between two lovers, Julie and St Preux (whom some suspect is based on Rousseau himself). St Preux is Julie's tutor and the book begins with his declaring his love for her. To his surprise, she returns his love, but Julie's father opposes their relationship and St Preux leaves for Paris. After the death of Julie's mother, she marries another man, a man more virtuous than St Preux himself. Ten years later, after they have two children, St Preux returns. Though Julie is an entirely devoted wife and mother, she can never forget her love for him, even in the events leading up to her tragic death at the end of the novel.

One interesting point about *Julie*, especially given is its very large public success among those in a society whose morals Rousseau thought corrupted, is how Rousseau can reconcile himself as an author when he has so sternly criticized the arts. The *First Discourse* (as well as the *Second Discourse*), his operas and the *Letter to D'Alembert* had already been published before *Julie*. Given the very strong criticisms in these earlier works, some have therefore brought the charge of hypocrisy against Rousseau. Based on the preface to *Julie*, it seems Rousseau was aware of this seeming contradiction and tried to address it. It opens with the following line: 'Great cities must have theatres; and corrupt peoples, Novels. I have seen the morals of my times, and I have published these letters. Would I had lived in an age when I should have thrown them in the fire!'[18] He later says that the book will not be enjoyed by people 'of taste' perhaps indicating that the substance of *Julie* is not in line with the corrupt morality of the day. Whether one buys Rousseau's explanation here or not, it is obvious that the tension of writing a product of art given his earlier philosophical work was not lost on him.

I believe, however, that this tension is far less interesting than the ways in which the characters in the novel represent and exemplify Rousseau's overarching philosophical system. I would like to take up just a few of them here, some pointing to parallels with the *First Discourse* and *Letter to D'Alembert*, which we discussed above, and others in connection with other works we shall examine in future chapters of this book.

Rousseau's suspicion of and disdain for urban environments clearly come through in *Julie*. It is no coincidence that the two lovers, both of whom exhibit virtue, are writing letters at the foot of the Alps. Their story could not have taken place in Paris. Further evidence for this is the fact that when he leaves the Alps and goes to Paris, St. Preux is miserable. As we have seen, Rousseau's general contempt for urban environments is a major theme in both the *First Discourse* and *Letter to D'Alembert*. In later chapters we shall see Rousseau argue the same theme, especially in the *Emile*, in which he claims that a pupil must be raised in the countryside to protect his moral character.

The notion of feminine virtue, a major area of interest among those studying Rousseau, is expressed in *Julie* as well. In the *Emile*, the character of Sophy is specifically identified as the paradigm example of a virtuous woman. As we shall see in Chapter 4, Rousseau's categorization of what a woman 'should be' is quite controversial. Nevertheless, the same philosophical account he gives in the *Emile* is represented by the character of Julie. For example, in the *Emile*, Rousseau claims that women are generally less apt for theoretical study of philosophy and science than they are for matters of practical study like morality. And similarly, in one of his letters, St Preux explains why as her tutor he has limited her field of study to stories of good taste and morality: 'Do not therefore wonder at the abridgements I am making in your earlier readings; I am convinced that they must be reduced in order to make them more useful.'[19] Feminine virtue, as we saw in the *Letter to D'Alembert*, is based in modesty. Recall that plays that over-emphasized a woman's intelligence or wit were damaging. Similarly Julie's modesty is described as virtuous.

Finally, the faculty of sentiment is emphasized in *Julie*. I will make mention of it here only briefly, and make a point of pointing out that sentiment is one of the most important aspects of Rousseau's thought. The most explicit account of sentiment (sometimes called pity) are in the *Second Discourse*, which we shall examine in the following chapter, and the fourth book of the *Emile* in a subsection on metaphysics and philosophy of religion titled *The Profession of Faith of the Savoyard Vicar*. Sentiment is a natural faculty, one that speaks through conscience, and which is indispensible for virtue. In *Julie*, it plays an important role. Take the following passage as just one example: 'If you followed your own rules; if in matters of sentiment you listened solely to the inner voice, and your heart silenced your reason, you would give in without scruple to the sense of security it inspires in you, and you would not attempt, against its testimony, to fear a peril that can come only from it.'[20]

These of course are only a few examples, and *Julie* is a work that has an enormous amount of secondary literature devoted to it. As my task in this book is to elucidate Rousseau's philosophical ideas, I have not addressed the many interesting and prevailing literary debates surrounding it. However, my general hope in this admittedly short section is to demonstrate that it is not, because it is a novel, unrelated to Rousseau's philosophy. And it is certainly very interesting to see Rousseau present some of these ideas in a different context.

v. CONCLUSION

These three works, *The Discourse on the Sciences and Arts, The Letter to D'Alembert* and *Julie or the New Heloise*, are all distinct and important in their own right. However, I have attempted to show how some of the more general themes of Rousseau's philosophy run through them. Most notably, we have seen in all three pieces that Rousseau is suspicious of so-called 'progress' whether it takes the form of scientific and artistic advances, the theatre or life in the urban modern city environment. Far from improving morals and virtue, these advances can often distract us and sometimes even corrupt us. Rousseau will develop the reasoning for these claims further in other works in a very robust and original conception of human nature. This conception and the arguments for it are presented in large part in the *Discourse on the Origin of Inequality*, which is the subject of the following chapter.

CHAPTER 3

THE STATE OF NATURE AND HUMAN HISTORY

i. INTRODUCTION

This chapter focuses exclusively on one text, the *Discourse on the Origin and Foundations of Inequality Among Men*, which is also referred to as the *Second Discourse*. This work, published in 1755, appeared 5 years after *Discourse on the Sciences and the Arts*. As we noted in the previous chapter, both works were responses to essay contests from the Academy of Dijon.

The question posed by the Academy this time was the following: 'What is the origin of inequality among men, and is it authorized by the natural law?' Rousseau's answer to this question, which would become the *Second Discourse*, did not win the Academy's prize as the *First Discourse* had several years earlier. In fact, in large part due to its length, it is reported that the judges at the Academy did not even finish reading it. However, as Rousseau was now a very well-known and widely read author, he was able to have the *Second Discourse* published independently. The work is interesting for several reasons and is undoubtedly one of the most important in Rousseau's corpus. In one sense, it is important because it picks up on several of the key themes articulated in the *First Discourse*. There (as we saw in the previous chapter), Rousseau is extremely critical of contemporary society. In the *Second Discourse*, we get much more in the way of a robust philosophical defence of those same criticisms. Furthermore, we see the emergence of several themes that would ultimately come to form the foundations of

Rousseau's political thought in the *Discourse on Political Economy* and *The Social Contract*, as well has his philosophy of education, ethics and metaphysics in *Emile*.

Before moving to a discussion of the *Second Discourse* itself, it will be helpful first to examine the Academy's question in a bit more detail, specifically, the point on whether inequality is authorized by the natural law. 'Natural Law' has a very particular meaning in the western philosophical tradition, and as a theory it has a very rich history. Of course, like any such theory, the term has come to be used in a variety of ways, and there is probably not one definition of it upon which everyone would agree. Nevertheless, we should say a few things generally about natural law theory so as to see where Rousseau is coming from in answering the Academy's question.

Perhaps the most influential version of traditional natural law theory is inherited from St Thomas Aquinas (Hobbes too is considered to be doing natural law theory, though as we will see his account differs from this traditional version). Aquinas, following Aristotle, argued that the most important aspect of any substance (humans, animals, plants, etc.) is its end or final cause. That is, by nature, everything is designed with a specific purpose; nature is neither random nor accidental. For Aquinas, the natural law is in part the rules and actions that human beings must follow if they are to properly follow their natural function, and part of that natural function is to live in society with one another. In societies, as we observe, some people rule and others are ruled. There is inequality of power and influence among the people of a given society. But if living in societies is part of our natural function; if *by nature* living this way is what are supposed to be doing, it could be argued on the grounds of natural law theory that inequality is in fact authorized by the natural law. Aquinas' writings came to form the basis of many philosophical positions of the Catholic Church, which of course had a great deal of power and influence in France during Rousseau's time. In the *Second Discourse*, one of Rousseau's primary objectives seems to be a railing of sorts against such a natural law argument, and hence the work was quite controversial. Rousseau argues conversely that natural inequalities are extremely minute and thus cannot be justified.

The *Second Discourse* is divided into four main parts, a dedication to Geneva, a preface, and two sections that compose the majority of the discourse itself simply referred to by Rousseau as the First Part and the Second Part. I have divided this chapter according to those parts, dedicating a section to the dedication and preface, as well as a section for each subsequent part of the discourse.

ii. THE DISCOURSE ON THE ORIGIN OF INEQUALITY

Rousseau's Dedication to Geneva and Preface

The *Second Discourse* begins with a dedication to Rousseau's birth-place, the Republic of Geneva. The overwhelming theme in the work is that the inequality established among people in contemporary society is not rooted in the fundamental nature of human beings. Rather, inequalities (of wealth, power and social status) are the result of a very peculiar series of historical events; but by nature, we are equal. When one reads the dedication, it is clear that Rousseau sees in Geneva a place in which the natural equality of human beings is largely preserved; or at the very least, Geneva is closest real life example to an ideal society. He states:

> While seeking the best maxims that good sense could dictate concerning the constitution of a government, I was so struck to see them all in practice in yours that even had I not been born within our walls, I should have believed myself unable to dispense with offering this picture of human society to that people which, of all others, seems to me to possess society's greatest advantages and to have best prevented its abuses.[1]

As the dedication continues, Rousseau continues along this line, claiming that had he been able to choose the place in which he was to be born, it would have all the characteristics of Geneva.

Rousseau's description of Geneva foreshadows several other major themes he argues for at length in the *Second Discourse* itself as well as in later political writings. A people should be free as they are in Geneva; but not free in the sense of having an individualistic license to do whatever one pleases. Rather they are free in the sense that the sovereign and the people are one that is the people in effect rule themselves.[2] The Republic gives great authority to its magistrates, electing those with the wisdom and virtue to legislate in ways that are truly for the benefit of all and trusting that they will do so. Geneva, unlike past societies such as Athens and Rome, has successfully avoided the danger of electing magistrates who rule with more of an interest in their own advancement than in the common good of the whole people. Thus, the magistrates rule for the sake of the people and so it is really the people who are ruling themselves.

It is interesting to speculate on how Rousseau would regard twenty-first century society in this respect. How, for example would Rousseau view politicians? Or perhaps more importantly, how would he view the disillusionment and pessimism with which most people regard politicians today? If I were to take a guess, I would imagine that Rousseau would not have so much praise for us. We see our magistrates, our elected officials, as dishonest; as 'flip-flopping' between issues, saying whatever they think they need to say to get votes; as making personal attacks on each other through 'mud-slinging' campaigns. Even for the citizens themselves, there is a prevalent view that many individual voters base their votes much more on what will benefit them individually than on what they perceive to be genuinely in the best interest of the society as a whole. Now it is by no means obvious or fair to make a blanket statement like this about *all* politicians, nor about *all* voting citizens. But, we are all certainly well aware of the stereotypes and there is certainly at least some truth in them.

Having praised Geneva as the ideal example of a government that preserves and celebrates the equality and goodness inherent in our nature, Rousseau then goes on to discuss his own father as a specific example of one of its virtuous citizens:

> My father, I joyfully admit it, was not distinguished among his fellow citizens: he was only what they all are; and such as he was, there is no country where his company would not have been sought after, cultivated, and even profitably by the most respectable men. It does not behoove me and, thank heaven, it is not

necessary to speak to you of the consideration which can be expected from you by men of that stamp: your equals by education as well as by the rights of nature and of birth; your inferiors by their will and by the preference they owe your merit, which they have accorded it, and for which you owe them in turn a kind of gratitude.[3]

Sadly, the praise Rousseau gives here to his father combined with earlier statements in the dedication about the constant wisdom, love and support his father gave him in his youth are likely exaggerated. By the time he was 12 years old, his father had abandoned him and left Geneva.

He continues with a tribute to the theologians of Geneva, 'whose lively and sweet eloquence carries the maxims of the Gospel the better into hearts as the pastors always begin by practicing them themselves'.[4] He speaks in this passage of how the spirit of Christianity is evident in Geneva's ministers, and of their example of the perfect unity of this spirit and the State. This general theme of religion would appear again in *Emile*, specifically in the 'Profession of Faith of the Savoyard Vicar', which we examine in detail in Chapter 4.

The dedication concludes with praise for the women of Geneva. As he did in the *First Discourse*, Rousseau looks to Sparta as an example and cites the fact that Spartan women were permitted to command; Genevan women deserve to command in Geneva as well. Furthermore, Geneva's virtuous women are free of vain luxury and 'maintain always by [their] amiable and innocent dominion and by [their] insinuating wit, love of laws in the State and concord among the citizens'.[5] He identifies women as the guiding conscience for men, and as the 'chaste guardians of morals'.

The picture of Geneva that Rousseau paints in this dedication is certainly a rosy one. When one reads it, she is led to believe that Geneva is the perfect society, almost a kind of heaven on earth. But Geneva, obviously, was not perfect and Rousseau was almost certainly well aware of this. In the notes to his and Judith Master's translation to the *Second Discourse*, Roger Masters writes, 'The style of the dedicatory epistle is marked by an often extravagant rhetoric, but beneath the glowing praise of Geneva Rousseau clearly delineates the requirements for the best regime a philosopher could wish for. A complete analysis of this dedication would indicate the extent to which these requirements were not fulfilled by Geneva in the eighteenth century.[6] So while much of what Rousseau sees in Geneva may be nostalgia for his homeland, or perhaps even a sense in which Geneva is far closer to what he perceives as the ideal political regime than other eighteenth-century societies, it should not be understood as an accurate representation.

The Preface to the *Second Discourse* follows the dedication to Geneva. A read of the preface can be particularly helpful to those approaching the *Second Discourse* for the first time, as it outlines in brief the major themes that follow in the discourse itself. Once again, the Academy's proposed question for the essay contest: 'What is the origin of inequality among men; and is it authorized by the natural law?' Some scholars rightly point out the fact that Rousseau spends the vast majority of the *Second Discourse* exploring the first part of the question, namely the origin of inequality, and significantly little time explicitly discussing the relation to the natural law.

The question of the origin of inequality among men, Rousseau tells us, is very difficult to answer, and the main reason why it is so difficult is that to answer it sufficiently, we would need to fully understand human nature itself. Obviously, the question 'What is human nature?' is an extremely broad and seemingly impossible question for any one, philosopher or not. But here, Rousseau has in mind one specific kind of difficulty that the question poses, and when one understands it, it becomes much easier to understand the *Second Discourse* and to appreciate what exactly Rousseau is up to. In short, the problem is that we have no way of observing what we might call 'pure' human nature. Now you might say, of course we can observe pure human nature, we need only look at ourselves and all those we interact with. But, for Rousseau, none of the people you would be observing would be a genuinely 'pure' subject. This is because so much of what we would be observing in these people (and even in ourselves!) would not be what we are by our nature that is at our *core*, but rather the result of learned behaviours and attitudes that we began acquiring from as early as our births. Hence, in the preface, Rousseau asks:

> Thus I consider the subject of this Discourse one of the most interesting questions that philosophy might propose, and unhappily for us, one of the thorniest that philosophers might resolve: for how can the source of inequality among men be known unless one begins by knowing men themselves? And how will man manage to see himself as nature formed him, through all the changes that the sequence of time and things must have produced in his original constitution, and to separate what he gets from his own stock from what circumstances and his progress have added to or changed in his primitive state?[7]

As we shall see below, a significant portion of the *Second Discourse*, indeed most of the first part, is devoted to answering this difficult question, namely: 'What is human nature strictly speaking?'

In formulating an answer to the question, Rousseau employs a strategy that was common to several other prominent thinkers in the seventeenth and eighteenth centuries. In short, the method is to 'strip away' all the attributes of human beings that are the result of society's influence. To better understand this, take a very simple example. Suppose I wanted to know what was common to all human beings, regardless of where and when they were living. I would not do very well to simply examine the people in my own particular society and assume that all of their attributes were part of this nature. Imagine that upon my observations, I noticed that nearly everyone in my society was able to use computers. I could not very well say that computer literacy was part of human nature. At best, I could only say that there was some cognitive potential in human beings that, should they live in a society with computers, could be actualized. But then it would be this mysterious potential in which I was interested, which in itself has nothing necessarily to do with computers at all. Now obviously, in the not too distant past, there were no computers and so no one was 'computer literate'. But of course we would not want to say that these people, nor those who live in other parts of the world in which there are no computers, are not 'human!' Rather, we would say that computer literacy is an accidental quality of human beings, one that many people in current day society happen to have, but one that they do not *necessarily* have in virtue of being human.

Now the example of computer literacy is a bit extreme, and one that I do not think anyone would seriously consider as an attribute of human nature. However, I believe it is useful to consider examples like these to see why Rousseau thinks the question of pure human nature is such a difficult one. If one stops and thinks about it, it is no easy task to come up with faculties, attributes or attitudes that are not the result of living in one's society. But that is only part of the problem. For in order to get to the root of human nature in itself, as Rousseau seeks to do, it would not even be enough to find traits that were common to human beings in *all* societies; because even these traits might nevertheless be the result of the mere fact of being in any sort of society whatsoever.

The project of defining human nature, as well as the method of 'stripping away' all of society's influences, had been taken on by other philosophers of whose work Rousseau was well aware. Typically these authors attempted to hypothesize about a 'state of nature'. That is, in their effort to conceive human beings apart from any of the artificial (for lack of a better term) influences of society, they imagined human beings with *no society at all*. They considered what life would be like, what would motivate such human beings, and how those human beings would relate to one another. Despite their efforts, however, Rousseau has this to say about these writers:

> The philosophers who have examined the foundations of society have all felt the necessity of going back to the state of nature, but none of them has reached it. Some have not hesitated to attribute to man in that state the notion of the just and unjust, without troubling themselves to show that he had to have that notion or even that it was useful to him. Others have spoken of the natural right that everyone has to preserve what belongs to him, without explaining what they meant by *belong*. Still others, giving the stronger authority over the weaker from the first, have forthwith made government arise, without thinking of the time that must

have elapsed before the meaning of the words 'authority' and 'government' could easily exist among men.[8]

Key here is the notion of previous philosophers feeling the necessity to describe the state of nature but failing to reach it. One of the philosophers that Rousseau undoubtedly has in mind here is Thomas Hobbes (1588–1679), who is one of Rousseau's major targets in the body of the *Second Discourse*. A brief discussion of Hobbes' view of the state of nature, and thus *human nature*, will be helpful, I believe, in elucidating key elements in Rousseau's view. In some ways, Hobbes serves as a perfect foil to Rousseau in this respect.

Hobbes' account of the state of nature is given most famously in his masterpiece the *Leviathan*, though he gives a similar account in *De Cive*. When Hobbes considers human beings outside of civil society, what he sees are creatures that are motivated purely by self-interest and who will stop at nothing to satisfy that interest. Why does Hobbes paint such a seemingly pessimistic view of human nature? His general answer looks like this. Hobbes' central point, with which Rousseau will actually agree in a sense, is that human nature is *not* social. Such a claim goes against the traditional philosophical worldview in the seventeenth and eighteenth centuries that was inherited from the ancient and medieval periods with Aristotle and Aquinas as its most famous advocates. For example, Aristotle begins his *Politics* with the statement that human beings are not merely naturally social, but indeed more social than any other animal in nature. Hobbes disagrees with this as the fundamental starting point for political philosophy, and to a large extent ethics as well. Instead, Hobbes describes society as a human *invention*:

The greatest part of those men who have written aught concerning commonwealths, either suppose, or require us, or beg of us to believe, that man is a creature born fit for society. The Greeks call him ζῷον πολιτικόν; and on this foundation they so build up the doctrine of civil society, as if for the preservation of peace, and the government of mankind, there were nothing else necessary, than that men should agree to make certain covenants and conditions together, which themselves should then call laws. Which axiom, though received by most, is yet certainly false, and an error proceeding from our too slight contemplation of human nature. For they who shall more narrowly look into the causes for which men come together, and delight in each other's company, shall easily find that this happens not because naturally it could happen no otherwise, but by accident.[9]

If society is an invention, as Hobbes claims in the above passage, then it makes sense to talk about the time before the invention.

To continue with the use of the example of computers that I mentioned earlier, we can talk about the period before we had computers. We could talk about the various historical circumstances that led to computers being invented, and we could easily conceive of the fact that it is possible that if some of these circumstances would have been different, computers could have easily not have been invented at all.

According to Hobbes, the period before society is the state of nature. To imagine what this state is like, we must take away all the parts of the invention. There would be no government, no laws, no industry and no culture. In short there would only be solitary individuals looking out for their own survival. To use a contemporary expression, the state of nature would be the paradigm case of 'survival of the fittest'. Hobbes himself describes the state of nature as the most horrible state of war: the war of every man against every other. We might think of it quite literally as a complete civil war. He famously describes life in the state of nature as 'solitary, nasty, brutish, and short'. Such a life is not an enviable one. Imagine constantly looking over your shoulder, never knowing when someone might take things from you, harm you or even kill you, and having no recourse to prevent it except what you yourself can provide. It is not a state in which most of us would want to live, and society is invented precisely because of this. For Hobbes, people realize that they have a better chance to survive and meet their needs if they 'cut their losses' in a sense. That is, they form a covenant with one another, agreeing on certain rules to follow in exchange for protection from each other. Society is invented because each individual realizes it is in her interest to join such a covenant, not because there is any genuine concern for the well-being of others or a noble sense of justice. Hobbes states:

> The final cause, end, or design of men, who naturally love liberty, and upon themselves, and dominion over others, in the introduction of that restraint upon themselves, in which we see them live in commonwealths, is the foresight of their own preservation, and of a more contented life thereby; that is to say, of getting themselves out from that miserable condition of war, which is necessarily consequent, as hath been shown, to the natural passions of men, when there is no visible power to keep them in awe, and tie them by fear of punishment to the performance of their covenants.[10]

The drive toward self-preservation is at the root of human nature for Hobbes, and ultimately leads human beings, though fear of one another, to leave the state of nature in favour of civil society. I think it is very helpful to keep the Hobbesian conception of the state of nature in mind when one approaches the *Second Discourse*. In an important way, Rousseau's task is to provide an alternative account to Hobbes, one which does not reduce human nature purely to self-interest. He seeks to provide an argument that human nature is not intrinsically 'evil' as Hobbes had claimed.

To this end, Rousseau outlines an important point at which his own view departs from that of Hobbes in the preface. While he agrees that human beings are motivated in large part by self-preservation, he believes that that self-preservation is not the *only* motivation we have:

> Leaving aside therefore all scientific books which teach us only to see men as they have made themselves, and meditating on the first and simplest operations of the human soul, I believe I perceive in it two principles anterior to reason, of which one interests us ardently in our well-being and our self-preservation, and the other inspires in us a natural repugnance to see any sensitive being perish or suffer, principally our fellow-men. It is from the

conjunction and combination that our mind is able to make of these two principles, without the necessity of introducing that of sociability that all the rules of natural right appear to me to flow.[11]

Perhaps the biggest difference between Hobbes and Rousseau with respect to their views of human nature is what Rousseau here describes as our 'natural repugnance to see any sensitive being suffer or perish'. This principle, which Rousseau will later in the *Second Discourse* term 'pity', is indispensable for explaining our progression from the state of nature to present day civil society. Having laid down his basic goals, Rousseau begins with the first of two parts of the *Discourse on the Origin of Inequality*.

The First Part

Rousseau must do two things, hence the first and second parts of the *Second Discourse*: he must give a description of human beings in their natural state, and he must then explain the events that caused human beings to move from that original state to our current one. The First Part describes the state of nature, and what Rousseau thinks constitutes *our* nature. Again, the best way to understand what he is doing is to think of 'stripping down' human beings of all those attributes that are the result of society's influence.

As stated above, Rousseau departs from accounts of human nature in the natural law tradition which begin with the foundational claim that humans are, by their nature, social. Like Hobbes, Rousseau, will argue that society is an invention. Now this may rightly strike one as puzzling. Certainly we observe other animals that seem, by their nature, to be social animals. For example, wolves travel in packs. Would we want to say that long ago wolves were solitary animals, but through historical circumstances or their own volition, they 'invented' the pack societies in which they now live for some perceived benefit? This would be odd. I think instead we would simply say that wolves *are social by nature*. We've never observed them otherwise. But why not say the same thing about humans? What is Rousseau up to here? I think Timothy O'Hagen gives a thoughtful answer to this question, which I'll borrow here:

> What sense does it make to hypothesize the existence pre- or sub-social human beings when all human beings do in fact live in societies? Scientists studying other species allow that some species are, and some are not, essentially social. So why should we not assume, as Aristotle and the natural law tradition does, that human beings, like ants, simply are essentially social? As I understand him, Rousseau is arguing that we should cast skeptical doubt on at least two received doctrines concerning essential human characteristics, the Aristotelian assumption of natural sociability and the Hobbesian assumption of natural aggression. Instead we should adopt the working hypothesis that the human raw material is almost totally malleable by its social environment . . . But the human raw material is not totally malleable.[12]

And so while Rousseau goes into great detail in the First Part of describing the state of nature, he should not be understood as claiming that there actually was some point in history in which the state of nature actually existed. The state of nature, instead, should be understood as a kind of thought experiment in which Rousseau shows that certain characteristics that we observe in civilized human beings could have, under different circumstances, been quite different.

Rousseau begins the First Part considering what man (to remain consistent with Rousseau I will often use the word 'man' although it is probably more appropriate to simply think in terms of 'humans' – both male and female) would be like in a physical sense. In fact, he goes into a fairly good amount of detail in this discussion, which might seem strange on one's first reading given that Rousseau states, 'I shall not stop to investigate in the animal system what he could have been at the beginning in order to become at length what he is. I shall not examine whether, as Aristotle thinks, man's elongated nails were not at first hooked claws; whether he was not hairy like a bear; and whether, if he walked on all fours . . .'.[13] Rousseau seems to be advocating something in the way of an evolutionary account, and despite what follows in his description of how man subsists in the state of nature, he nevertheless ignores how man's physical attributes may have been very different. Why does he ignore these seemingly important issues? Once again, it is important to note that Rousseau's task is not primarily concerned with the details of evolutionary biology (a discipline that did not even exist at the time he wrote the *Second Discourse*); rather, in his own words, his task is to '[strip] this being . . . of all the supernatural gifts he could have received and all of the artificial faculties he could have only acquired by long progress'.[14] When Rousseau pictures man in the state of nature, who he refers to throughout the text as 'savage man', he pictures a being that is basically the same as you or I physically: walking on two legs, equally vulnerable to disease and physical harm, having the same sensory faculties, etc.

My own view for why Rousseau believes it is necessary to give the following account of 'savage man in the physical sense' is because he is anticipating a possible objection from his readers. The objection goes something like this: it makes no sense to think of a man living by himself in the forest without the protection, advantages and comforts society provides. Take any man out of society, strip him naked, take away all his possessions, put him in the woods, and he will be lucky to survive for more than a few days! Rousseau, therefore, must give an account that shows that it is a least *plausible* that creatures more or less equal to us physically could survive in just this way, both as individuals and as a species.

While Rousseau agrees that 'plucking' civilized man out of society and inserting him in the wilderness would almost certainly result in a quick death, he disagrees that this is the proper way to imagine savage man. We might say that society has made us soft:

Accustomed from infancy to the inclemencies of the weather and the rigor of the seasons, trained in fatigue, and forced, naked and without arms, to defend their lives and their prey against other wild beasts, or to escape by outrunning them, men develop a robust and almost unalterable temperament. Children, bringing into the world the excellent constitution of their fathers and fortifying it with the same training that produced it, thus acquire all the vigor of which the human species is capable.[15]

Savage man has never known shelter, or tools, or help from his fellow man, and so all he has known since his birth is solitary life in the wilderness. In fact, Rousseau says, if we take away tools and weapons, a fight between savage man and civilized man would be very one-sided! Furthermore, savage man is certainly well equipped enough to pass his days in the state of nature without fear of other animals like wolves or bears. On the occasions in which he encounters such predators, he sometimes runs away, and sometimes fights them off.

Despite his rough exterior and his ability to survive in the state of nature, however, Rousseau says that it would be a mistake to think that, at his core, savage man is violent or aggressive. Instead, following Montisquieu, Cumberland and Pufendorf, he argues '. . . that nothing is so timid as man in the state of nature'.[16] Here is one of the first key passages in which Rousseau is careful to distinguish his account of natural man from that of Hobbes, who as we saw above, saw the state of nature as the most violent state of war. Instead of seeing conflict everywhere, and an existence filled at every moment with either violence or the threat of violence, Rousseau sees the state of nature as tranquil and peaceful; encounters with others are rare, and there is an abundance of goods (which for savage man are very basic and relatively few) available for everyone.

The other major threat Rousseau identifies in the state of nature for human beings is disease. He once again says that many of our health problems are ironically the *result* of society, rather than alleviated by it:

> . . . excess of idleness in some, excess of labor in others; the ease of stimulating and satisfying our appetites and our sensuality; the overly refined foods of the rich, which nourish them with binding juices and overwhelm them with indigestion; the bad food of the poor, which they do not even have most of the time, so that their want inclines them to overburden their stomachs

greedily when the occasion permits; late nights, excesses of all kinds, immoderate ecstasies of all the passions, fatigues and exhaustion of mind; number-less sorrows and afflictions which are felt in all conditions and by which souls are perpetually tormented: these are the fatal proofs that most of our ills are our own work, and that we would have avoided almost all of them by preserving the simple, uniform and solitary way of life prescribed to us by nature.[17]

Once again, I think it is helpful to keep in mind what Rousseau is trying to do in these passages, namely, give an explanation as to how humans could survive in the state of nature as he has described it. So, if one were to argue that without modern medicine, or at the very least the help of others, human beings' susceptibility to disease would make survival impossible, the above would be Rousseau's response. Furthermore, we observe many animals in nature that show a resiliency in this respect. Rousseau mentions cats, bulls and horses as a few examples. All of these animals, he argues, become far *less* resilient once we have domesticated them; why, then, should we think human beings any different?

Having given a description of what savage man is like physically, the remainder of the First Part of the *Second Discourse* is dedicated to a far more ambitious and more specifically philosophical task. In Rousseau's words, 'let us look at him from the metaphysical and moral side'.[18] What follows are some of the most key tenets in Rousseau's thought, not only in the central theses of the *Second Discourse*, but which also play a crucial role throughout many of his later works which followed.

It seems very much to this point that savage man is no different than any other animal. Indeed, Rousseau has been arguing that we must be careful not to attribute to him any of those faculties that could only have arisen from societal conventions. This extends even to the most basic reasoning skills. He 'sees him satisfying his hunger under an oak, quenching his thirst at the first stream, finding his bed at the foot of the same tree that furnished his meal; and therewith his needs are satisfied.'[19] Savage man has no language, no association with others, nor any real concept of the past or future, not even his own death: '. . . because an animal will never know what it is to die; and knowledge of death and its terrors is one of the first acquisitions that man has made in moving away from the animal condition'.[20] But are human beings substantially different in some way from other animals? For Rousseau, undoubtedly, yes, they are. However, if one were to have the perspective of some outside observer on the state of nature, she would not see this. She would not see anything in savage man's outward behaviour that would make her take note and say, 'Aha! This animal is importantly different than all the others!' Humans are distinct from all non-human animals, but the difference lies in faculties that are completely underdeveloped in the state of nature.

Like other animals, human beings possess two principles, to which we saw Rousseau refer in the Preface: self-preservation and pity. Recall that these two principles are anterior to reason. Self-preservation, the principle on which Hobbes based his account of human nature, is I think fairly straightforward. One need not look very hard at both humans and not humans alike to see that they take great pains to maintain their lives. The second of these principles, pity, Rousseau had earlier categorized as a 'natural repugnance to the suffering of others'. This principle, though not unique to human beings, is key in understanding the core of many of what we call virtues in civil society. A more thorough account of pity is given below.

In addition to the principles of self-preservation and pity, Rousseau argues that human beings have two further faculties that distinguish him from all other animals, though they are in a sense dormant in the state of nature: freedom and *perfectibility*. Let us now treat Rousseau's discussion of these.

The debate over free-will is one of the most prevalent in philosophy. At the risk of being anachronistic, Rousseau's view on the topic is, by contemporary terms, probably best understood as libertarian.[21] Though human beings sometimes act on instinct, simply reacting to external stimuli, they can refuse these impulses or give into them. They can *choose* to do otherwise. A further account of how, or at the very least why, Rousseau believes this is given in *Emile* in the *Profession of Faith of the Savoyard Vicar*. We'll examine this account in the next chapter. The following excerpt explains Rousseau's basic position as it is given in the *Second Discourse*:

> In every animal I see only an ingenious machine to which nature has given senses in order to revitalize itself and guarantee itself, to a certain point, from all that tends to destroy or upset it. I perceive precisely the same things in the human machine, with the difference that nature alone does everything in the operations of a beast, whereas man contributes to his operations by being a free agent. The former chooses or rejects by instinct and the latter by an act of freedom, so that a beast cannot deviate from the rule that is prescribed to it even when it would be advantageous for it to do so, and a man deviates from it often to his detriment.[22]

It is interesting that Rousseau does not distinguish humans from non-humans by saying that we have reason whereas they do not: 'it is not so much understanding that which constitutes the distinction of man among the animals as it is his being a free agent'.[23] We differ from animals not in terms of having categorically different sensory experience and ideas than they do, but rather in having these experiences and ideas to a higher degree. Freedom, according to Rousseau, lies in the ability of humans, and humans alone, to in a sense 'break away' from nature. His evidence for such a claim is largely empirical. If we simply examine the world around us, we will observe that humans are the only species that adapts and changes. With non-human animals, if something is not rooted in their natural instinct, their 'hard-wiring' as it were, they will never be able to realize it: 'Thus, a pigeon would die of hunger near a basin filled with the best meats, and a cat upon heaps of fruits or grain, although each could very well nourish itself on the food it disdains if it made up its mind to try some.'[24] Rousseau's discussion of freedom leads him to the second unique faculty of human beings, *perfectibility* (also referred to at some points as 'self-perfection').

The transition from freedom to perfectibility in the *Second Discourse* is a bit ambiguous, and it is not immediately clear where one begins and the other ends. For after using examples like the cat and the pigeon to illustrate how a being without freedom cannot go against or break from what it is programmed to do by instinct, Rousseau then suggests:

> . . . if the difficulties surrounding all these questions [of freedom] should leave some room for dispute on this difference between man and animal, there is another very specific quality that distinguishes them and about which there can be no dispute: the faculty of self-perfection, a faculty which, with the aid of circumstances, successively develops all the others . . .[25]

Perfectibility seems to be defined here as that faculty that enables human beings, both as individuals, and as a species to change over time that is to move further and further from nature. Individuals learn things, change their habits and adapt to new situations. The human species continues to do these things on a large scale, and as a species we often like to marvel at the 'progress' we have made through history. Rousseau explains, '. . . an animal is at the end of a few months what it will be all its life and its species is at the end of a thousand years what it was the first year of that thousand.'[26] If, according to Rousseau, freedom is defined as the ability to act against or outside of natural instinct, and perfectibility is defined as moving away from nature, what precisely makes them two distinct faculties? The simplest answer, I think, is this. Freedom is the capacity to, should a situation present itself in which the agent takes it to be advantageous, to go against instinct. If a cat only had fruits and grains available to it to eat, it would require a free act to go against instinct and eat these foods. Perfectibility, however, must be linked in some intimate way to consciousness. If the cat freely ate the fruits and grains, but was not conscious that he was doing so, he would likely not eat fruits and grains again unless a similar situation presented itself. Free acts without at least some rudimentary form of consciousness cannot lead to permanent changes and adaptations. Human beings are both free and have an innate ability to *know* they are acting freely. Hence they can incorporate these freely chosen acts into their lives, and indeed can do so collectively in groups, through generations.

Despite savage man's possession of these faculties, Rousseau makes clear that they rely on chance circumstances to be, for lack of a better term, 'awakened:' 'Whatever the moralists say about it, human understanding owes much to the passions, which by common agreement also owe much to it. It is by their activity that reason is perfected; we seek to know only because we desire to have pleasure; and it is impossible to conceive why one who had neither desires nor fears would go to the trouble of reasoning.'[27] One might contrast Rousseau's position here with the famous opening line from Book I of Aristotle's *Metaphysics*: 'All men by nature desire to know. An indication of this is the delight we take in our senses; for even apart from their usefulness they are loved for themselves.'[28] Reason does not awaken in savage man because of some innate and genuine intellectual curiosity; reason is triggered by some new situation that forces savage man to reject instinct when he cannot satisfy some need that he previously had no difficulty satisfying. This point, too, Rousseau claims can be supported empirically: '. . . the peoples of the North are more industrious than those of the South because they can less afford not to be, as if nature thereby wanted to equalize things by giving to minds the fertility it refuses the earth.'[29] Human beings in the state of nature, have only the most basic needs, and given what Rousseau has just said about reason, it is evident that were those needs met, they would *never* leave the state of nature. The following passage, I believe, is one of the most eloquent in all of Rousseau's writings:

Should we want to suppose a savage man as skillful in the art of thinking as our philosophers make him; should we, following their example, make him a philosopher himself, discovering alone the most sublime truths and making for himself, by chains of very abstract reasoning, maxims of justice and reason drawn from love of order in general or from the known will of his creator; in a word, should we suppose his mind to have as much intelligence and enlightenment as he must and is in fact found to have dullness and stupidity, what utility would the species draw from all this metaphysics, which could not be communicated and which would perish with the individual who would have invented it? What progress could the human race make, scattered in the woods among the animals? And to what point could men mutually perfect and enlighten one another, who, having neither fixed domicile nor any need of one another, would perhaps meet hardly twice in their lives, without knowing or talking to each other.[30]

The meaning of this quote is basically that philosophy could not develop unless it was *useful*; and it would certainly not develop without society. Rousseau goes on in considerable detail to describe how much of what we may now consider to be the most basic of faculties are in fact extremely complex. Rather than thinking they are part of human nature, and thus properties of savage man, he argues to the contrary that they would take an enormous amount of time to come about.

The faculty Rousseau discusses in the most detail is the use of language. He provides a quite lengthy discussion of how long it would take for even the most basic language to come about. And, in keeping with what we have just seen above, this development takes place out of necessity, not because of some innate desire to communicate or some intellectual curiosity. The first words were merely grunts and cries; when savage man began naming objects, he would give a proper name to everything. Rather than looking at two oak trees and calling them both 'oak trees', he would likely call one A and the other B. Abstracting from these particulars to form a general concept that they are 'the same thing' cannot possibly come until much later in the development of language.

Having established savage man from the 'metaphysical' perspective as a very simple being with very simple needs, Rousseau then considers him from the 'moral' point of view. This discussion also constitutes Rousseau's most explicit response to Hobbes. As savage man is motivated in large part by a drive to preserve himself, we saw Hobbes conclude that he must be 'naturally evil'. That is, he is aggressive and violent particularly when it comes to dealings with his fellow man. By contrast, Rousseau argues that savage man is not naturally evil; he is best considered as an amoral being:

It seems at first that men in that state, not having among themselves any kind of moral relationship or known duties, could be neither good nor evil, and had neither vices nor virtues ... Above all, let us not conclude with Hobbes that because man has no idea of goodness he is naturally evil; that he is vicious because he does not know virtue; that he always refuses his fellow-men services he does not believe he owes them; nor that, by virtue of the right he reasonably claims to things he needs, he foolishly imagines himself to be the sole proprietor of the whole universe. Hobbes saw very clearly the defect of all modern definitions of natural right; but the consequences he draws from his own definition are no less false. Reasoning upon the principles he establishes, this author ought to have said that since the state of nature is that in which care of our self-preservation is the least prejudicial to the self-preservation of others that state was consequently the best suited to peace and the most appropriate for the human race. He says precisely the opposite, because of having improperly included in the savage man's care of self-preservation the need to satisfy a multitude of passions which are the product of society and which have made laws necessary.[31]

I take Rousseau to be saying that even if Hobbes is right about savage man at the metaphysical level, namely that he is motivated purely by self-preservation, we would still not be compelled to accept the claim that he is naturally aggressive, violent and evil. Those capacities, as they are manifested by human beings in civil society, require far too much in the way of complex rational processes that, like language, would have taken an enormous amount of time to develop.

But Rousseau goes further; not only is Hobbes wrong about what a being motivated solely by self-preservation would be like, but he is also wrong that self-preservation is savage man's only guiding principle. As we saw above in the earlier discussion of the Preface to the *Second Discourse*, Rousseau sees another faculty in human beings: pity. In that passage, we saw pity defined in short as a 'natural repugnance to the suffering of another'. In the First Part of the *Second Discourse*, Rousseau discusses pity in more detail and argues that it is fundamental for understanding basic human nature as well as many aspects of human beings in civil society, especially those attributes to which we typically refer as virtues.

Rousseau states:

> There is besides, another principle which Hobbes did not notice, and which – having been given to man in order to soften under certain circumstances, the ferocity of his vanity or the desire for self-preservation before the birth of vanity – tempers the ardor he has for his own well-being by an innate repugnance to see his fellow-man suffer. I do not believe I have any contradiction to fear in granting to man the sole natural virtue that the most excessive detractor of human virtues was forced to recognize. I speak of pity, a disposition that is appropriate to beings as weak and subject to as many ills as we are; a virtue all the more universal and useful to man because it precedes in him the use of all reflection.[32]

Pity in natural man is a basic reaction to suffering and is, as Rousseau says at the end of this passage, 'unreflective'. He notes that other animals exhibit this principle as well; horses are hesitant to trample another living body, and cows utter a sad lowing when they enter a slaughterhouse and observe the horrible sight of what's inside.

Rousseau uses a particularly gripping example when it comes to human pity, borrowing from Mandeville's *Fable of the Bees*. Imagine an imprisoned man forced to watch a wild beast tearing a child from his mother's breast and violently killing the child as the mother watches helplessly. What would the imprisoned man feel as he watched this? He would undoubtedly be distraught and horrified. Rousseau poses the following observation: 'What horrible agitation must be felt by this witness of an event in which he takes no personal interest!'[33] When we witness suffering, even when that suffering is in no way a threat to ourselves, and even when those suffering are perfect strangers to us, we feel pity.

Now of course one might try to salvage a Hobbesian account and explain our feelings of pity as, in fact, more complicated expressions of self-preservation. We might say, on such an account, that when one witnesses suffering the visceral reactions we have are due to our putting ourselves in the person's place. So when I see someone suffering, at a subconscious level, I think to myself 'That person is suffering greatly. I can imagine myself suffering that way, and I would certainly want to avoid such suffering, and hence this unpleasant feeling arises in me.' But is this Hobbesian reply plausible? I believe Rousseau would say that it is not, and those sympathetic to it are making the mistake of ascribing very complex and abstract reasoning skills to savage man: skills that could only have come about over a long period of time and socialization.

But it would be a mistake to call savage man 'virtuous' because he feels pity. Once again, we must remember that pity is in itself unreflective, and that savage man is an amoral being, neither virtuous nor vicious. Nevertheless, pity allows civilized human beings, after reason has been triggered and developed, to be virtuous. So while it does not make savage man good, it makes goodness *possible*. Rousseau states:

> . . . even with all their ethics men would never have been anything but monsters if nature had not given them pity in support of reason; . . . from this quality alone flow all the social virtues . . . In fact, what are generosity, clemency, humanity, if not pity applied to the weak, to the guilty, or to the human species in general? Benevolence and even friendship are, rightly understood, the products of a constant pity fixed on a particular object: for is desiring that someone not suffer anything but desiring he should be happy?[34]

Since Rousseau argues that human beings in the state of nature are good, it is often said that we must return to nature in order to be good ourselves. But this is not exactly right; savage man is not good in the moral sense. It may seem paradoxical, but savage man, though amoral, serves as a moral example to us. He does this in the sense that we risk having this natural principle stamped out in civil society, which we must guard against. The method for preserving pity in our current social existence is, in large part, the foundation of the educational programme laid out in *Emile*, which we will examine in the next chapter.

As we close this discussion of the First Part, it will be helpful to summarize Rousseau's basic account of human beings in the state of nature and once again consider his view of what we are at our core, stripped of all those qualities, attributes and abilities that we could only acquire with society's influence. Essentially, human beings are made up of four basic components. Two of these, self-preservation and pity, they share with other non-human animals. The other two, freedom and *perfectibility*, are uniquely human and make it possible for human beings to break from the state of nature and ultimately form society. Finally, we should note that Rousseau seems to have great praise, even a sense of longing, for the state of nature. Rather than seeing it as a miserable state of war like Hobbes, he says the following, which I think is an appropriate way to conclude our discussion of this section:

> Now I would really like someone to explain to me what type of misery there can be for a free being whose heart is at peace and whose body is healthy? I ask which, civil or natural life, is most liable to become unbearable to those who enjoy it? We see around us practically no people who do not complain of their existence, even many who deprive themselves of it insofar as they have the capacity: and the combination of divine and human laws hardly suffices to stop this disorder. I ask if anyone has ever heard it said that a savage in freedom even dreamed of complaining about life and killing himself. Let it then be judged with less pride on which side true misery lies. Nothing, on the contrary, would have been so miserable as savage man dazzled by enlightenment, tormented by the passions, and reasoning about a state different from his own.[35]

The Second Part

Recall that the question posed by the Academy concerns the nature of inequality and whether it is in accordance with the natural law. The First Part of the *Second Discourse*, as we have just seen, 'proved that inequality is barely perceptible in the state of nature, and that its influence there is almost null'.[36] Without social relationships, the only inequality that exists between humans in the state of nature are those that are purely physical; one person might be slightly stronger or faster than another. But of course such inequalities are very minimal, and indeed Rousseau says that even if they did allow one person to dominate another, the domination would only last until the stronger turned away for a moment, and the other person simply runs away never to encounter him again.

In civil society, however, there are vast inequalities among human beings, and the majority of them are not physical but rather social, economic or political. One of the fundamental aspects of civil society that allows these inequalities to come about is the notion of property: a notion that is completely foreign to savage man. Rousseau begins the Second Part with the following statement: 'The first person who, having fenced off a plot of ground, took it into his head to say *this is mine* and found people simple enough to believe him, was the true founder of civil society.'[37] Rousseau then adds that had someone stood up to this 'imposter' and told the others that such a claim was illegitimate that 'the earth belongs to no one', the human race would have been spared 'crimes, wars, murders, miseries, and horrors'.

It is obvious that savage man did not simply decide to fence off a plot of land one day and invent private property. Though we can imagine such an event happening very long ago, there must have been a great many events leading up to it. The Second Part of the *Second Discourse* is in large part a hypothetical account of events that took savage man in the pure state of nature to civilized man in something resembling present-day society. Rousseau does not claim that things necessarily progressed in exactly the way he describes them, but does claim that roughly speaking, the story he tells is the most probable account.

Perhaps the best way to understand Rousseau's discussion in the Second Part is as a series of stages. The first is the pure state of nature, which is the account we have just examined as Rousseau presents it in the First Part. The last stage is civil society. Of course by civil society Rousseau is referring to his own society, most notably eighteenth-century France. Although, more than 250 years have passed since Rousseau wrote the *Second Discourse*, I have always been struck by how well his observations, criticisms and insights remain strikingly relevant to our own society as well.

Following author Timothy O'Hagen, I believe the progression to take place through seven distinct stages (though our current society is only the sixth).[38] In the account I give below, I will use O'Hagen's terminology though I should emphasize for the sake of clarity that these are not Rousseau's explicit terms and Rousseau himself does not formally divide his account into these specific stages. Nevertheless, I think proceeding in this manner is the best way for those unfamiliar with the *Second Discourse* to understand the key elements of the Second Part. The designated stages are: (1) Nascent Man – The Pure State of Nature; (2) Elementary Cooperation – The State marked by Hunting, Gathering and Fishing; (3) The 'Youth of the World' – The Stone Age; (4) Nascent Society – The Iron Age; (5) The State of War; (6) Civil Society – Current Day Society which is marked by injustice, inequality and despotism and (7) A New Civil Society – A Future or at least Potential Society that is marked by justice and equality.

Stage (1), the Pure State of Nature, is simply savage man as Rousseau describes him in the First Part of the *Second Discourse*. He is motivated by self-preservation, but is tempered by pity. He has the faculties of freedom and perfectibility but these faculties are as yet un-awakened, and thus reason remains completely undeveloped. He is an amoral being that is neither good nor evil properly speaking. He has no language, no concept of others, no social relations, very little reflection and lives a simple and relatively basic existence. Perhaps the most important thing to note about the nature of the transitions between the various stages is that they (especially the early ones) are caused by external chance events. As reason develops and social relations increase in the later stages, the transitions come to be caused more directly by the wills of people themselves.

The transition between stage (1) and stage (2) Elementary Cooperation is caused primarily by climatic changes. O'Hagan notes Rousseau's mention of long summers and winters, as well as the chance discovery of fire as the external events that led to this transition. These climatic changes necessitated the very beginnings of savage man breaking from pure instinct to act freely, though the actions were motivated by the principle of self-preservation. When I picture examples of how this would have happened, I always imagine a savage man who had always found food in a given place in the forest. However, due to a harsh climate, the food is no longer within his reach, and so he uses a stick or some other primitive tool to acquire it (something the pigeon would never be able to do). Hence Rousseau states 'Along the sea and rivers they invented the fishing line and hook, and became fisherman and eaters of fish. In forests they made bows and arrows, and became hunters and warriors. In cold countries they covered themselves with the skins of the beasts they had killed.'[39] In addition to these technological advances, the State of Elementary Cooperation is also marked by the first social interactions of savage man with other human beings like himself. These interactions are, of course, very basic, though Rousseau claims that through such interactions savage man begins to judge that his fellows' ways of thinking and feeling are similar to his own. The interactions are normally centred on a particular task (Rousseau's example is that of hunting a deer) and they last only as long as it takes to complete that task. Furthermore, if one of those involved takes it to be in his interest to leave the group, leave his post as it were, he would do so with no regret or guilt. Thus, even in these social interactions, human beings remain largely amoral.

Rousseau maintains that 'These first advances [those from stage (1) to stage (2)] finally put man in the position to make more rapid ones.'[40] The more rapid changes to which Rousseau is referring are those that mark the transition from the State of Elementary Cooperation to stage (3) The Youth of the World. As use of tools increases, human beings begin to build huts, which led to a basic idea of property as well as a differentiation of families. The association that human beings had with one another also led to a real awareness of others, a moral sense of entitlement and pride, as well as a sense of comparing oneself with others. This notion of comparison, of having love for oneself out of a sense of superiority to another, is the basis of an unnatural self-love that Rousseau terms *amour-propre*. *Amour-propre* is discussed at length in *Emile*, and we will devote significant space to it in the following chapter. Especially in the *Second Discourse, amour-propre* is put forth in a very negative light, and it can, if unchecked, cause a great deal of misery. But we must stop short of saying that *amour-propre* is intrinsically wrong or harmful. The Youth of the World is a collection of families, living among one another, and interestingly, is the stage in which we find 'most of the savage peoples in the world' according to Rousseau. Whatever one may want to say about the historicity of the *pure* state of nature, Rousseau is advocating here that this relatively early stage in the transition from the state of nature to that of civil society is empirically observable. It is also noteworthy that Rousseau calls this stage, The Youth of the World, the happiest for human beings, a kind of 'happy medium' between the pure state of nature and current-day civil society:

> Thus although men had come to have less endurance and although natural pity had already undergone some alteration, this period of the development of human faculties, maintaining a golden mean between the indolence of the primitive state and the petulant activity of our vanity, must have been the happiest and most durable epoch. The more one thinks about it, the more one finds that this state was the least subject to revolutions, the best for man.[41]

The familial relationships in The Youth of the World lead to conjugal love between husbands and wives, and paternal love of parents for their children. Rousseau calls these the two sweetest sentiments known to men. Rousseau's praise for this stage in human history rests, I think, on the fact that much of nature's innocence is preserved. Despite new feelings of pride, some competition among human beings, and even property disputes, this stage remains the best for man. Why? Because despite these new potential dangers that are absent in the Pure State of Nature, there is relative equality among the people. Some may be slightly stronger or cleverer; some might have slightly nicer huts; however, all are equal in the sense that each can satisfy all his needs (which are relatively few and simple) by himself. Thus, Rousseau explains:

> As long as men were content with their rustic huts, as long as they were limited to sewing their clothing of skins with thorns or fish bones, adorning themselves with feathers and shells, painting their bodies with various colors, perfecting or embellishing their bows and arrows, carving with sharp stones a few fishing canoes or a few crude instruments; in a word, as long as they applied themselves only to tasks that a single person could do and to arts that did not require the cooperation of several hands, they lived free, healthy, good, and happy insofar as they could be according to their nature, and they continued to enjoy among themselves the sweetness of independent intercourse.[42]

Only a 'chance accident' can explain the transition out of this stage to stage (4) Nascent Society – The Iron Age. It is not so much the accidents themselves that cause the transition, but rather the discovery of two arts that result from them: agriculture and metallurgy. Rousseau thinks some accidental event is the only plausible explanation as to why these arts would be undertaken. He considers metallurgy first. Why would it ever occur to human beings in The Youth of the World to try to melt down metal and form new tools and weapons? '. . . it is necessary to suppose in them much courage and foresight' to undertake such difficult labour and to envisage so far in advance the advantages they could fain from it: all of which hardly suits minds that are not already more trained than theirs must have been.'[43] Therefore, Rousseau ponders, the discovery and practice of metallurgy must have been caused by something external, something out of the ordinary: hence, a 'chance accident'. Perhaps a volcano eruption allows human beings to observe metallic materials and it occurs to them to attempt to imitate the practice. Likewise agriculture likely came about as an art once other arts allowed for large scale cultivation of the land.

The primary reason that Rousseau equates the arts of metallurgy and agriculture with an important transition in human history is because the practice of these arts made it no longer possible for each individual to meet his own needs. These arts are specialized and required the division of labour. And so, some men were needed to smelt the iron, others were needed to till the land, etc. Men no longer 'did a little of everything' simply to meet their own needs, but rather focused on doing one task or occupation, and exchanging their labour with others to meet their other needs. Labour is at the core of our contemporary notion of property rights and justice:

> From the cultivation of land, its division necessarily followed; and from property once recognized, the first rules of justice. For in order to give everyone what is his, it is necessary that everyone can have something; moreover, as men began to look to the future and as they all saw themselves with some goods to lose, there was not one of them who did not have to fear reprisals against himself for wrongs he might do to another. This origin is all the more natural as it is impossible to conceive of the idea of property arising from anything except manual labour.[44]

Even with this division of labour, Rousseau posits, things could have remained equal if talents had been equal. But of course some perform their work very well and others struggle; suddenly some people have a great deal of property and others very little. We can see here how the gross inequality of which Rousseau is so critical depends on labour. As we saw in the First Part, there are very small inequalities among men in the state of nature, but once the division of labour becomes a part of society, those small inequalities become magnified. And once this happens, conflicts begin to arise.

The escalating conflicts and violence among human beings, some of them with much and some of them with little, marks stage (5) The State of War. Rousseau discusses this stage rather briefly, but one is reminded once again of the Hobbesian account of the state of nature. However, for Rousseau, The State of War is very far removed from The Pure State of Nature, a state to which it was impossible to return:

> Between the right of the stronger and the right of the first occupant there arose a perpetual conflict which ended only in fights

and murders. Nascent society gave way to the most horrible state of war: the human race, debased and desolated, no longer able to turn back or renounce the unhappy acquisitions it had made, and working only toward its shame by abusing the faculties that honor it, brought itself to the brink of its ruin.[45]

In Hobbes' account of human beings coming out of the state of war, which was the original state of nature, people decide that it is in their self-interest to give up their right to any and all things in exchange for the protection they gain from a social contract. The social contract, therefore, according to Hobbes, is a legitimate and advantageous institution far preferable to the state of nature. Rousseau, however, tells a far more insidious story. The social contract is in fact nothing more than a trick; it is a deceptive way for those with the most to lose to convince those who are worse off to maintain the present inequality:

> To this end, after having shown his neighbors the horror of a situation that made them all take up arms against one another, that made their possessions as burdensome as their needs, and in which no one found security in either poverty or wealth, he easily invented specious reasons to lead them to his goal. "Let us unite," he says to them, "to protect the weak from oppression, restrain the ambitious, and secure for everyone the possession of what belongs to him. Let us institute regulations of justice and peace to which all are obliged to conform, which make an exception of no one, and which compensate in some way for the caprices of fortune by equally subjecting the powerful and the weak to mutual duties. In a word, instead of turning our forces against ourselves, let us gather them into one supreme power which governs us according to wise laws, protects and defends all the members of the association, repulses common enemies, and maintains us in an eternal concord."[46]

It may seem strange when reading the above passage that Rousseau thinks that the social contract described here is specious and deceptive. After all, a set of rules that 'makes an exception of no one' and 'defends all members' seem to be elements of a society that most of us would want to put in place. But, keep in mind that these rules are only put in place *after* arbitrary inequalities have taken hold. The powerful have far more to lose than the poor by having them in place, and so it is much more in their interest to advocate them. The poor, however, also live in fear and wish to have an alternative to the state of war. The alternative is appealing, and they do not realize that they are sealing their fate as a lower class of people. Once the social contract is in place, it serves only to maintain the injustices that already existed. Hence, without realizing it, the poor 'ran to their chains', ensuring their unjust second-class status would remain permanent. Rousseau remarks, 'The poor having nothing else to lose except their freedom, it would have been great folly for them to give away voluntarily the sole good remaining to them, gaining nothing so to speak in exchange'.[47]

Of course a long time has passed since this last transition took place from the State of War to the State of Civil Society. And a great deal has changed; nations have come and gone, new discoveries have taken place, technological advances have been made, etc. Nevertheless, in terms of our position relative to our purely natural state, and in terms of the inequalities among human beings, we remain under this specious social contract.

The final stage (7), A New Civil Society, is Rousseau's vision of what a legitimate social contract would be, and some of his most famous political philosophical insights focus on it. We will discuss these at length in Chapter 5. In the *Second Discourse*, however, Rousseau says the following:

> If we follow the progress of inequality in these different revolutions, we shall find that the establishment of the law and of the right of property was the first stage, the institution of the magistracy the second, and the third and last was the changing of legitimate power into arbitrary power. So that the status of rich and poor was authorized by the first epoch, that of powerful and weak by the second, and by the third that of master and slave, which is the last degree of inequality and the limit to which all the others finally lead, until new revolutions dissolve

the government altogether or bring it closer to its legitimate institution.[48]

Rousseau has now sketched an account of the source of inequality in human society, but it is not until the last few pages that he addresses the Academy's second question: whether inequality is ordained by the natural law. Not surprisingly, Rousseau argues that inequality is almost non-existent in the state of nature, and thus no one is *by nature* superior or inferior to anyone else. Inequality 'draws its force and growth from the development of our faculties and the progress of the human mind, and finally becomes stable and legitimate by the establishment of property and laws. It follows, further, that moral inequality, authorized by positive right alone, is contrary to natural right whenever it is not combined in the same proportion with physical inequality . . . [inequality in society] is manifestly against the law of nature'.[49]

Like the *First Discourse*, the *Second Discourse* is extremely critical of commonly accepted notions of current day society, in this case, the social structure that allows for vast inequalities among its people. Rousseau is not only arguing that these inequalities are unjust, but is also saying not all that indirectly that any philosophical system that claims they are legitimate, such as traditional natural law theory, is dubious.

iii. CONCLUSION

The *Second Discourse* is an important text for a number of reasons. For one thing, it generated a controversial response from its readers, though it would certainly not be the last of Rousseau's works to have such an effect. However, it is a prime example of a work that put Rousseau in between traditional and enlightenment camps. His defence of the natural goodness of human beings was at odds with the Church's doctrine of original sin. However, his praise of savage man and indictment of civil society was clearly counter-enlightenment. One of the more noteworthy reactions to the *Second Discourse* came from Voltaire, who called it a 'work against the human race'. He also added sarcastically that the work inspired him to want to start crawling around on all fours like an animal. However, since he had not done such a thing since he was a baby, he felt it was a habit to which he could not go back.

Controversy aside, I think the *Second Discourse* also forms a crucial point in the development of Rousseau's thought. There are themes in it that were originally developed, though less rigorously, in the *First Discourse*. And, conversely, some of the more fundamental aspects of Rousseau's philosophical system (humans' natural goodness, the injustice of inequality, amour-propre versus amour de soi, etc.) are first mentioned here before becoming fully developed in later works like *Emile* and *The Social Contract*. These developments will in large part be the subjects of the following chapters.

CHAPTER 4

PHILOSOPHY OF EDUCATION

i. INTRODUCTION

Emile or 'On Education' was published in 1762 (the same year as his major work in political philosophy *The Social Contract*) and is considered one of Rousseau's most important works. At the time of its publication, it was also one of his most controversial. *Emile* was immediately banned by Parisian authorities (as was *The Social Contract*), and Rousseau needed to flee France to avoid arrest. As we shall see in the discussion of Book Four below, Rousseau's views on religion denied basic tenets of the Catholic Church.

Upon picking up the book for the first time, one of the most striking things about it is its enormous size, over 500 pages.[1] The title of the book is perhaps a bit misleading. Although it is in large part a book on education, it is also a great deal more than that. It has been rightly categorized as a hybrid of sorts: it is both a work on education as well as a work on philosophy; it is both a treatise and a novel; and it is partly a work of fiction and partly auto-biographical. These various lines are woven together throughout, and although it can be somewhat confusing to a reader approaching it for the first time, I believe that these different approaches actually enrich and even enliven the text. Perhaps it will be helpful to briefly spell out these different angles and the fundamental question/s with which each is concerned.

As a work of education, Rousseau is concerned with articulating the most effective way of teaching a student. While he does discuss conventional aspects of education, such as math and history, he is more concerned with moral education; teaching a child to be 'good'. As a work of philosophy, Rousseau continues to explore the basic theme that humans are not evil by nature, and he investigates the possibility of a person being good despite living in a corrupt society. Additionally, in Book Four, we get Rousseau's most explicit discussion of the relationships between metaphysics, morality, God and religion. As a novel, the book tells the story of Emile, who is raised by his tutor from birth until his marriage in his early twenties. But as a treatise, there are extensive passages that make no mention at all of Emile or the characters in his life. And finally, the work is fictional that it is a hypothetical account of someone educated by nature; but it is told in the first person, with Rousseau assuming the role of Emile's tutor. Though the tutor is a fictional character in one sense, Rousseau often tells anecdotes from his own life, his own education and his own experiences educating others. In this sense, the work is also autobiographical, although at many points it is not easy to distinguish between the fictional and the autobiographical.

At the risk of oversimplifying, if we were to try to tie all these aspects of *Emile* together, I think they point us to one fundamental question: 'How can one be good in an evil world?' Each of the different perspectives speaks to this question in a unique way. *Emile* is divided into five books, and I have divided this chapter into sections corresponding to each of them. Rousseau also wrote the beginning of a sequel to *Emile*, called *Emile and Sophy*. I have included a short discussion of this work as well.

ii. THE EMILE

Book One

Book One begins with a discussion of Rousseau's basic educational project in *Emile*. The goal, ultimately, will be to show how to raise a child from birth to adulthood. The result will be a man who is 'well-educated' in the sense of being a thoughtful and independent person; but even more importantly, he will be properly educated in the moral sense. To do this, Rousseau's educational programme seeks as much as is possible to imitate a child's natural upbringing. In this respect, *Emile* works in large part from several of the basic tenets for which Rousseau had argued in the *Second Discourse*. As we discussed in the previous chapter, it would of course be impossible to combat society's ills by attempting to return to a pure state of nature. We cannot 'un-trigger' reason, unlearn language or undo the social relationships in which we are now entrenched. Nevertheless, many of savage man's characteristics, if cultivated in a civilized human being, would make him virtuous. Recall that savage man is robust and strong, peaceful, relatively free of anxiety and completely oblivious to what others think of him. A civilized man, even in a society like eighteenth-century France which Rousseau sees as corrupt (recall his criticisms of it especially in the first and second *Discourses*), would live quite happily if he possessed of these characteristics. Thus, the first line of *Emile* reads 'God makes all things good. Man meddles with them and they become evil'.[2] Proper education, for Rousseau, seeks to eliminate the conflict between what we are by our nature, and what society tells us we ought to be. In fact, Rousseau claims, we are taught by 'three masters': by nature, by men and by things. Nature is completely out of our control; we cannot change our nature anymore than we can change other elements of nature like laws of physics. 'Things' are partly under our control, they consist of experiences and our surroundings. But the education that comes to us from 'men' is totally within our control. Since the goal is nature, and nature is beyond our control, we must ensure that the two elements of education that we do have control of work to be in line with nature. A harmony of these three masters rather than a conflict is really what *Emile* is all about as a work of philosophy of education.

As we noted above, however, a complete return to nature is not possible. If human beings are going to live among one another, if they are to reason, indeed if they are to be 'moral creatures' properly speaking, they will have already gone against nature in some sense. So, the harmony of which Rousseau speaks here must be taken to mean harmony *as much as is possible*. One of the most significant points on which we must choose between nature and man is that of being a solitary individual versus being a citizen:

The natural man lives for himself; he is the unit, the whole, dependent only on himself and on his like. The citizen is but the numerator of a fraction, whose value depends on its denominator; his value depends upon the whole, that is, on the community. Good social institutions are those best fitted to make a man unnatural, to exchange his independence for dependence, to merge the unit in the group, so that he no longer regards himself as one, but as a part of the whole, and is only conscious of the common life.[3]

This concept of citizenship, of seeing oneself as part of community and a willingness to sacrifice one's individual interests for the good of that community, is one which Rousseau sees in Geneva (recall the dedication to the *Second Discourse*) and in historical examples such as the Spartans, whom of course he praised in other works as well, most notably the *First Discourse*. This same idea will form the foundation of his notion of the ideal political regime in the *Discourse on Political Economy* and *Social Contract*, which we will discuss in the following chapter.

The remainder of Book One focuses on education at the child's first stage, his infancy. It might strike us as odd that Rousseau would include a lengthy discussion of infant-care in a treatise on education, but we must keep in mind that education is not merely schooling, it is far broader than that. He begins by attacking what was the common practice of well to do families at the time a baby was born. At that time, wet-nurses were hired to care for and breast feed the baby. Babies were tightly swaddled, as it was thought that this would keep them from hurting themselves; however, many including Rousseau suspected that this was actually done so the nurses could more easily ignore the baby and leave it alone for long periods. At any rate, Rousseau argues adamantly that mothers should nurse their own children in part because it allows for an important emotional bond to form between mother and child. On this point, Rousseau seems quite progressive as such a claim is fairly uncontroversial nowadays. Furthermore, and this is a point to which Rousseau returns and emphasizes several times in Book One, infants should not be tightly swaddled. This is one specific example of how Rousseau uses nature as a guide for proper education. In nature, he argues, their limbs are free to move and exercise and the result is stronger and sturdier young children.

At the time Rousseau was writing, the customary means of education was, when the child was old enough, to hire a tutor to begin the child's formal education. Just as Rousseau argues that mothers, and not wet-nurses, should nourish their children, ideally it would be fathers, and not tutors, that educated them. He leaves this aside, however, and the remainder of *Emile* is based upon the tutor/pupil relationship. Interestingly, Rousseau makes a point of saying that he views himself as completely unqualified to actually put his own educational method into practice, and so is content merely to write it. One will no doubt recall that Rousseau sent his own children, all five of them, to an orphanage. The phrase, 'Those who cannot do, teach' is perhaps well apt in this case.

As always, Rousseau is careful to articulate how his means of education differs from those of the established method. Tutors should be assigned to their pupils very early, when they are still infants; to wait until the child is five or six is too late. The child's character has already been formed, and it is likely to be so flawed so as to make proper education impossible. Similarly, the tutor remains with the pupil throughout his entire childhood and even into early adulthood, and the book chronicles the tutor's relationship to the hypothetical pupil, Emile, through all these stages.

For the most part *Emile* is written in the first person, with Rousseau himself as the narrator who plays the role of tutor. The pupil, Emile, is first mentioned by name in Book One, though the references to him specifically are few until the later books. The 'hybrid' form of *Emile* as both treatise and novel, to which we referred above in the introduction to this chapter, is somewhat progressive, gradually moving from treatise to novel. Book One reads the most like a treatise with Rousseau pointing out flaws with education and arguing, based on nature, for alternative measures. But as *Emile* continues into books Two through Five, the story of Emile the character comprises more and more of the text. Emile is first mentioned as Rousseau explains what his pupil will be like. He will be born from a rich and well to do family, though he will be an orphan (perhaps so that Rousseau can more easily implement his programme without complicating it by discussing how the tutor will interact with Emile's parents). Emile will also be healthy. In rather cryptic terms, Rousseau claims that 'if you take the care of a sickly, unhealthy child, you are a sick nurse, not a tutor. To preserve a useless life you are wasting the time which should be spent in increasing its value, you risk the sight of a despairing mother reproaching you for the death of her child, who ought to have died long ago.'[4] It may seem as though Rousseau is being very callous and heartless in this remark, and in a sense such comments rightly seem to us to be simply indefensible. Nevertheless, Rousseau himself, I do not think sees it quite this way. Once again, the overriding theme is nature, and in nature, only the healthy and strong children survive past infancy. So perhaps the most charitable way to read Rousseau on this point is to say that the education of a natural man to live in society cannot be performed on unhealthy children. To give them the care that they need to survive would require us to move too far from nature to implement such an education. And this, I take it, is really what Rousseau means, not that a less than healthy child should simply be left to die.

The education of infants, what we now typically think of has early-childhood development, advocates many principles that are actually quite progressive and accepted by many people today. Other aspects, however, are likely to seem outrageous, though even these Rousseau will argue are ultimately rooted in nature.

One of the more noteworthy points Rousseau makes is that 'Men are devoured by our towns', through living so close together in dense populations. Nature intends instead, and once again we might recall the arguments regarding the state of nature in the *Second Discourse*, that human beings live scattered, dispersed, in more rural environments. Against the prevailing wisdom of the time, Rousseau argues that infants should be born outside of towns, and should be exposed to the fresh air and sunlight. Infants are completely devoid of any experiences, lacking even consciousness of their own existence. Their first experiences are pleasures and pains, but even these experiences are so basic that the children cannot differentiate between different pleasures and different pains, and

certainly cannot make causal inferences about the external circumstances that lead to them.

Education begins with habits according to Rousseau, and even
in the early stages before children can walk or talk, they can be
influenced by habits. Rousseau gives several examples as to how to
properly habituate young children, all aimed primarily at eliminating common fears that children have. Children are afraid of
spiders, masks and loud noises like thunder. However, if we first
show the child masks that are not scary and gradually show him
more and more frightening masks all the while laughing at them,
even the most hideous mask will only make the child laugh. If we
expose him to spiders, to the sound of gunshots, always in a gradual
way without showing fear ourselves, the child will never develop
these common fears. The notion of habituation will play an enormous role in the educational programme throughout childhood,
and we will see it invoked in numerous ways in the later books
of *Emile*.

At first, children simply have no language but their cries, and
before they have been habituated their cries always indicate a
legitimate need. But very early on, they begin to acquire a sense
of power that they wish to exercise; they begin to test those
around them, crying when they simply want to command. Knowing
when to respond to the cries and when not to is one of the key
elements of education during this early stage. If we do not respond
enough, the child becomes desperate, but if we respond too often,
the child becomes a tyrant. Thus, Rousseau cautions, 'Study carefully their speech and gestures, so that at an age when they are
incapable of deceit you may discriminate between those desires
which come from nature and those which spring from perversity'.[5]
Once the child has moved from the newborn stage to the beginnings
of walking and talking, he has moved to the next phase of his life.
Therefore, the next stage of his education must begin. For in addition to these new abilities, the child has formed a rough idea of
himself, and has developed the beginnings of reason and a moral
character.

Book Two

Book Two focuses on the next stage of the pupil's life, his childhood. Roughly speaking, Rousseau considers this stage to last between the ages of 2 and 12 years old. The specific references to Emile increase in Book Two. Additionally, Book Two gives accounts of Rousseau's own experiences teaching children. In these accounts, the children are often quite headstrong and difficult thanks to the flawed education they have previously received. Rousseau remains true to the educational programme set out in Book One, carefully articulating how the strategies used ensure that the pupil remains close to nature. The key to this, which Rousseau emphasizes throughout the second book, is to allow the child to learn by experience, and to seek out knowledge on his own because *he* has seen the value in it.

First and foremost, Rousseau argues that childhood ought to be fun. While he is of course concerned that Emile will learn valuable lessons and develop, he is extremely cautious about overwhelming him with formal training that the child will find tedious and boring. If we know one thing with certainty about human life, Rousseau says, it is that it can be taken at any time. We all think it is tragic when children die, but it is much more tragic if the child spent the entirety of his short life being bombarded with books and schooling: all of this preparation for an adulthood that the child never reached. Rousseau is exaggerating a bit here, but the point is that learning ought to be fun for the child. Thus, Rousseau puts all of Emile's lessons in the context of experience, and specifically childlike experience, using games, adventures, etc.

The goal of education, as we have seen, is more than merely an acquisition of knowledge. Ultimately the goal is to develop the whole person, and to make the pupil happy. Rousseau explains happiness in general terms as the equality of one's desires with one's powers. A being who had the power to fill all his desires would be 'perfectly happy'. Why does Rousseau have so much praise for natural man, the savage? Because the savage has only the most simple and basic desires, desires that are easily satisfied. It is true that as society progresses we acquire a great many comforts and knowledge, but with all these advances come desires which become increasingly more difficult to satisfy. This conflict is the basis of our unhappiness. Even our fear of death (which Rousseau says is foreign to savage man in the *Second Discourse*) gives rise to such unhappiness. Rousseau is critical of doctors throughout Emile, and one of the main reasons for his animosity is that doctors make us fear all of the various ways that our health can suffer. They make us terrified of what could go wrong in the future, which of course is always uncertain anyway. To put it simply, ignorance is bliss; and worrying about the future is a fruitless exercise.

But this general point about happiness with regard to the relationship between desires and powers has other implications for education. Rousseau states, 'There is only one man who gets his own way – he who can get it single-handed; therefore freedom, not power, is the greatest good. That man is truly free who desires what he is able to perform, and does what he desires. This is my fundamental maxim. Apply it to childhood, and all the rules of education spring from it.'[6] Freedom, or liberty, consists of independence, of self-reliance. Liberty is achieved, therefore, by eliminating dependencies. Rousseau says dependencies come in two forms: 'those based on things' which are natural and 'those based on men' which are unnatural. An education based in nature seeks as much as possible to eliminate dependencies on men, which Rousseau says gives rise to every kind of vice. When men come to depend on each other too much, they lose their liberty and become slaves to one another. And so, keeping Emile from becoming dependent on others ensures he will be free, happy and closer to nature.

Interestingly, Emile's moral education during his childhood is completely negative, meaning that the work of the tutor is to prevent him from being corrupted rather that attempting to teach him morality and virtue. Rousseau reiterates the claim he makes at the very start of *Emile* that 'the first impulses of nature are always right. There is no original sin in the human heart, the how and why of the entrance of every vice can be traced. The only natural passion is self-love or selfishness taken in a wider sense'.[7] This passage foreshadows many of the discussions that come later in the text. The denial of original sin plays a major role in the explanation of natural religion in the Profession of Faith of the Savoyard Vicar in Book Four, and the passion of self-love lies at the heart of the distinction between *amour-propre* and *amour de soi*; but we shall postpone these discussions for now. Children, according to Rousseau, are unable to grasp the true nature of morality. If the tutor tries to teach certain moral principles such as, 'Do not lie' or 'Do not take what does not belong to you' because 'it is wrong', the child will not take them to heart. In fact, the child is likely to try to break such rules simply for the sake of breaking them out of a sense of excitement or rebellion. But we cannot blame children for this, it is in the nature of children to act this way, and so we must work with nature rather than fight against it. And so not only is 'book-learning' tedious and unpleasant for children, it also fails to really teach them effectively.

Rousseau has a different means for teaching lessons of all sorts, including morality. In a word, the child must learn by *experience*. The tutor carefully constructs an environment in which the pupil can discover truths himself. There are several examples dealing with various lessons, so for the sake of brevity I will mention only one of them here. The following is how the tutor teaches Emile basic notions of property and justice.

The tutor takes Emile into the countryside. We should also note that, in staying close to nature, Emile spends his childhood in the country rather than the city. Recall the remark in Book 1, 'Men are devoured by our towns'. The tutor and Emile come upon a plot of land and the tutor explains that Emile can have this land and cultivate it. The tutor even volunteers to help Emile, to be his 'under-gardener' and together they plant beans, water them and care for them every day. Through the process of joining his labour to the land, Emile comes to really understand the notion of property. He feels a connection and even a right to his little garden. But one day, when Emile and the tutor come to the garden they find all the beans have been dug up. At first Emile is outraged that someone destroyed his property, the fruits of his labour. He and the tutor come to find out it was the gardener, Robert, who dug up the beans. But when Emile confronts Robert, he finds that the gardener had, long before Emile planted his beans, planted melons in the same plot of land. So ironically, it is Emile who must apologize for destroying Robert's property, and make things right; he now has a primitive sense of justice.

It is far easier for a child to learn about morality, specifically property rights and justice, through an experience like this with the garden rather than to simply read definitions of rights and justice in a book. Emile has discovered it himself in a very personal way and so he truly understands these notions. From a practical standpoint, it is obvious that the tutor must go to a good deal of trouble to set up these experiences for Emile. By Rousseau's own admission in the above lesson, for example, he needed to arrange things with Robert so as to stage the event. In other lessons, the tutor goes to similar lengths to teach the child. There is a large amount of deception in Rousseau's educational programme. The child has no idea that these forming experiences are in fact completely artificial, staged if you will. Rousseau does little in *Emile* as far as a formal justification for such deception, indicating that he probably did not think such measures were all that controversial, at least not to the point of making any qualifying remarks.

Teaching by experience, Rousseau says, must make use of our basic means of experience, sensation. In Book Two, he takes time to explain how each sense should be used in accordance with nature to further the child's knowledge. We allow the child to see the relationship between sight and touch, the two most important and constant senses, by presenting him with different objects. He then learns to approximate distances and even learns basic principles of geometry. Rousseau also speaks of a sixth sense, common sense, which 'has no special organ, it has its seat in the brain, and its sensations which are purely internal are called precepts or ideas. The number of these ideas is the measure of our knowledge; exactness of thought depends on their clearness and precisions; the art of comparing one with another is called human reason.'[8] As Emile continues to acquire basic ideas from sense experience through creative exercises and games, and to have other experiences that help him form abstract ideas such as basic moral concepts, reason develops. Furthermore, because the tutor is careful to let Emile at least think that he is largely in control of his own actions and the decisions he makes, he ensures that his pupil will preserve his natural sense of independence and hence his liberty.

Emile will not have the benefits of a so-called formal education; he may not be as 'book smart' as other children, but his moral character and his ability to think for himself and solve problems will be far superior:

His [Emile's] ideas are few but precise, he knows nothing by rote but much by experience. If he reads our books worse than other children, he reads far better in the book of nature; his thoughts are not in his tongue but in his brain; he has less memory and more judgment; he can only speak one language, but he understands what he is saying, and if his speech is not so good as that of other children his deeds are better.[9]

Emile's childhood, his negative education, has left him uncorrupted. Thus, he is prepared as he enters adolescence to begin a new phase of his education, which is the subject of Book Three.

Book Three

Book Three continues with the basic educational strategies outlined in Book Two, though Emile is now about twelve years old, so the lessons and subjects are more advanced. Rousseau's conception of happiness, as the desires not exceeding powers, gives the pupil a great sense of strength at this age. Previously, during childhood, Emile's life is marked by weakness. Though his desires are relatively few, he nevertheless needs a great deal of help in satisfying them. This all changes when he reaches the age of 12 or 13. At this age he gets much stronger physically and is now able to satisfy many of these desires by himself.

One notices, however, that despite this change in Emile, many of the same cautions are taken by the tutor to protect him from corruption. Ignorance is praised by Rousseau as being far superior to thinking one knows things of which he is in fact mistaken. In this respect, Rousseau follows Socrates, who famously said that the fact that he *knew he did not know* made him the wisest of all men.

Reason and judgement can only be developed slowly, and to rush them can lead one to many false ideas.

Rousseau continues to construct environments to allow Emile to have experiences that bring him to knowledge, or to make him yearn to acquire knowledge. These are similar in kind to the example of the garden that we touched upon in the preceding section. One of the cleverest in Book Three is used to help Emile gain an appreciation for the study of astronomy. The tutor and Emile take a hike into the woods. When it is noon, and they are ready to eat lunch, the tutor pretends that they are lost and do not know which way to go in order to get back to town. Emile initially is terrified and begins to cry. But after some questions about their previous day's observation of the sun as it relates to directions, Emile is able to figure out their location and get them back. He then remarks to his tutor 'come to dinner, make haste! Astronomy is of some use after all'.[10]

One of the major endeavours that marks this new stage in Emile's maturation process is labour. Not surprisingly, Rousseau praises those means of labour that are more rustic, as these he says are closer to nature. In the *Second Discourse*, we saw that Rousseau argues that the division of labour is a major turning point in the development of human society. People live relatively happily among one another before this happens, but when arts like metallurgy and agriculture come about, and labour becomes too specialized for each to provide for all her individual needs, some become masters and others slaves. This same sentiment is expressed in *Emile*:

The exercise of the natural arts, which may be carried on by one man alone, leads on to the industrial arts which call for the co-operation of many hands. The former may be carried on by hermits, by savages, but the others can only arise in a society, and they make society necessary. So long as only bodily needs are recognized man is self-sufficing; with superfluity comes the need for division, and distribution of labour, for though one man working alone can earn a man's living, one hundred men working together can earn the living of two hundred. As soon as some men are idle, others must work to make up for their idleness.[11]

Emile, like all his fellow citizens, is born into a society in which the division of labour has already taken place. Although the division of labour takes the human race further from nature, and this is regrettable in some sense, we cannot return to nature by eliminating it. The tutor must show Emile how to appreciate labour, and how to understand the way in which it makes some people rich and others poor. Once again, the best way to teach this lesson is through experience. Two experiences in particular are worthy of mention and each shows Emile a unique perspective about the value of different forms of labour.

The first lesson is learned when the tutor takes Emile to a fancy and extravagant dinner with very wealthy people. Before they go to the dinner, the tutor and Emile discuss the various arts and products in society. All of these substances, Rousseau explains, must be judged by their usefulness. Society has given us many prejudices in this respect and the result is that many of the things we value greatly are quite unnecessary. For example, we think that diamonds are more valuable than iron. But why should this be? Iron is far more useful to us. We might think diamonds are very beautiful, but ultimately they do not really make our lives any easier, or help us to build things, or to nourish ourselves. Our basic natural drive towards self-preservation is not really helped at all by having diamonds. Iron, however, is very useful. We can use it for all kinds of purposes that improve our lives. So the working of iron is a form of labour that is far closer to nature than the art of a jeweller: 'Goldsmiths, engravers, gilders, and embroiderers, he [Emile] considers lazy people, who play at quite useless games'.[12] Once Emile is able to see the natural, and true, way to value labour, he is then taken to dine with the rich. All around him, Rousseau tells us, Emile sees servants, elegant china, and expensive clothes. As he is taking all of this in, the tutor whispers to Emile to think about how many hands all these extravagant items must have passed through in their being manufactured. Emile will come to realize that these trivial luxuries required an enormous amount of labour; that 'every quarter of the globe has been ransacked that some 2,000,000 men have laboured for years, that many lives have perhaps been sacrificed, and all to furnish him with fine clothes to be worn at midday and laid by in the wardrobe at night'.[13] Rather than be impressed by the status symbols of the wealthy, Rousseau tells the reader, Emile will be repulsed by it and consider it frivolous and wasteful.

The second way Emile comes to learn about the value of labour and its relationship to nature is for him to learn a trade. Agriculture and metallurgy are the two labours closest to nature, but Rousseau chooses a third trade, carpentry, as that which Emile will learn: carpentry is far closer to nature than other trades like acting, embroidering or jewelling, which are not nearly as useful. The tutor will learn along with Emile, both will be apprenticed to the carpenter. Through his training, Emile will continue to learn the value of producing things with his own hands. Additionally, because the trade is practical and useful (hence it is close to nature), knowledge of this trade and the ability to supply oneself with basic needs that carpentry provides will limit his dependence. These lessons, which begun in Emile's childhood and which we saw and Book Two, become further solidified as he grows older.

Though Emile's formal education is still limited, he is now prepared to take steps to learn more about abstract topics. He has not been ruined by trying to teach these lessons too early. So he is ignorant, but like Socrates, is in a better position than most because he does not mistakenly think he knows things. He is now 15, no longer a child but not yet a man.

Book Four

As a work of philosophy, Book Four is arguably the most important in the *Emile*. Though Book Three ends when Emile is around the age of 15, Book Four skips ahead and often refers to him as a young man of 18 or 20. The discussion of the tutor's educational regime with Emile continues, but much of Book Four is somewhat divorced from the story. As the themes it presents are somewhat scattered, I think it will be helpful to generally state the main ideas here and then proceed by discussing each of them, as well as how Book Four is divided. As I read it, Book Four consists of three main parts. It begins by continuing where Book Three left off, discussing Emile's education. It is then interrupted by the Profession of Faith of the Savoyard Priest, a piece which could certainly stand on its own as an independent philosophical work on religion, ethics and metaphysics, though it is presented in the larger text of the *Emile* as an aid to show how to teach the pupil about religion. Following the Profession of Faith, Book Four continues the story of Emile.

Book Four is the longest in the *Emile*; it can (and has) had entire books dedicated to it, so obviously my treatment of it here must be somewhat limited. Nevertheless, the ideas expressed in it are some of the most eloquent, the most profound and the most discussed in all of Rousseau's thought. Preceding the Profession of Faith of the Savoyard Vicar, Rousseau discusses the beginnings of Emile's moral education, citing the role of the passions and their relationship to nature. He roots much of moral education on the two forms of self-love to which we referred in the last chapter on the *Second Discourse*: the natural form of love, 'amour de soi' and the unnatural form 'amour-propre.' The important role of the motivating principle of pity in morality is presented here as well. This discussion takes place in the context of Emile's education. Following it, the question is then raised as to the best way to teach him about religion. Rousseau, in a somewhat confusing and round about way, appeals to his personal experience with a young priest who instructed him about God, morality and the nature of religious belief. He claims to have transcribed the priest's words to him, and the resulting treatise the Profession of Faith. However, the account is fictional at least in the sense that the priest is a fictional character based on people influential in Rousseau's life. The claims made in it are best considered simply as Rousseau's own views on these topics. Following the Profession of Faith, in the continued discussion of Emile, we see how the pupil is introduced into society and how he begins to search for a woman to share his life with. The themes I have mentioned above are those I think most appropriate to focus on in my discussion of Book Four.

To love ourselves is one of the most fundamental aspects of our nature according to Rousseau, this point was made in the *Second Discourse* in his discussion of that first impulse in each of us that prompts us to take an interest in the preservation of our own life and well-being. Even savage man, in this basic sense, loves himself. He calls this principle of self-love, the natural form of self-love, 'amour de soi'. In the *Emile*, Rousseau states: 'The origin of these passions, the root and spring of all the rest, the only one which is born with man, which never leaves him as long as he lives, is self-love [*amour de soi*][14]; this passion is primitive, instinctive, it precedes all the rest, which in a sense are only modifications of it. In this sense, if you like, they are natural.'[15] At about the time Emile reaches puberty, he has what Rousseau calls the 'second birth' and he means by this that Emile's passions (we might also call them emotions) are awakened. The passions we feel are, according to the above quote, modifications of the natural faculty of self-love, *amour de soi*. It is the work of moral education to control these passions, but not to eliminate them; they cannot be eliminated and to try would be an impossible fight against nature. Emile's passions, which spring from his *amour de soi*, can be the foundation of social virtues if he is educated in the proper way. As nature 'makes all things good' *amour de soi* as a natural principle within us is also good:

> Self-love [*amour de soi*] is always good, always in accordance with the order of nature. The preservation of our own life is specially entrusted to each one of us, and our first care is, and must be, to watch over our own life; and how can we watch over it, if we do not take the greatest interest in it?[16]

Amour de soi, we might say, is an independent kind of self-love; it does not intrinsically depend on one's relationships to other people. Nevertheless, civilized human beings who have a developed sense of reason and reflection can have their *amour de soi* affected and even cultivated by social experiences. But at its root, *amour de soi* is simply a basic caring about oneself.

The second form of self-love, *amour-propre*, is unnatural because it is essentially social. It depends on one's relationship with other people and can easily become corrupted by feelings of competition and pride. Rousseau's transition from the discussion of *amour de soi* to *amour propre* is marked by caution.

Expand these ideas [of self-love] and you will see where we get that form of selfishness we call natural selfishness [*amour-propre*], and how selfishness ceases to be a simple feeling and becomes pride in great minds, vanity in little ones, and in both feeds continually at our neighbor's cost. Passions of this kind not having any germ in the child's heart, cannot spring up in it of themselves; it is we who sow the seeds, and they never take root unless by our fault.[17]

Rousseau's discussion of *amour-propre* throughout the *Emile* and other works as well such as the *Second Discourse* is overwhelmingly negative, or at the very least cautionary. Since *amour-propre* is a love of oneself that depends on others, it risks being corrupted into the social vices that Rousseau sees as plaguing society. Recall all of the societal problems he describes in the *First Discourse* as examples.

We can better understand this by way of example. Suppose that I want to be the best student in my class. I work hard, I take pride in it, and when I have academic success I, in a sense, 'love myself' for it. As long as the love I have for myself is rooted in my own abilities and achieving the goals I have set for myself, such a self-love is much closer to *amour de soi*, though of course savage man would not exist in a world of society much less a in world of schools and grades. But now suppose that I become so obsessed with being the best student in my class that I start taking great pleasure in the misfortunes of my fellow students. Every time one of them does poorly on an exam, though I might pretend to be sympathetic, I am secretly filled with glee. It gives me a sense of pride in myself, but the pride is largely rooted in my feeling of superiority over others. And if I had no fellow students, if I were simply studying independently, I would not be able to feed this pride anymore. Simply learning on my own and accomplishing individual goals would leave me feeling hollow, because I would not know that I had 'beaten' anyone else. So we can see how *this* type of self-love depends on my relationship to other people, thus it is unnatural; if unchecked, corrupted *amour-propre* can consume individuals, filling them with bitterness and vice towards others.

It might look as though Rousseau is simply saying that there are two forms of love, *amour de soi*, which is good; and *amour-propre*, which is bad. While it is true that *amour-propre* is almost always mentioned as something to be constantly checked and guarded against, it would not be correct to say that it is *intrinsically* bad. Amour-propre, as a faculty, is not a normative (that is neither good nor bad in itself) form of self-love. It is a way of regarding oneself that is 'other regarded'; *amour-propre* can have a positive outlet, and in the ideal political regime (see the following chapter on the *Discourse on Political Economy* and *Social Contract*) it can be a way of taking a healthy sense of pride in oneself based on the view that others take towards her. It can help one more steadfastly adhere to her duties and obligations as a citizen.[18] Despite this, however, a corrupted form of *amour-propre* can be devastating. In the corrupt society of eighteenth-century France, a society united by the specious social contract that Rousseau describes in the *Second Discourse*, this is most often the way that most people's *amour-propre* manifests itself. Protecting Emile from such corruption is perhaps the most crucial part of moral education. One of the primary ways to do this is to cultivate Emile's natural principle of pity, which we saw Rousseau describe in the *Second Discourse* as human beings' repugnance to the suffering of others. When reason is developed, pity becomes reflective, and we are able to put ourselves in the position of those who suffer. To ensure that we do this in a way that gives a genuine concern for others rather than through a corrupted form of *amour-propre*, Rousseau says there are three basic maxims to follow. In brief they are as follows:

1. We should aim to expose people to the suffering of others, those who will arouse our pity. This is because we put ourselves in the place of those who are worse off than we are, not those who we perceive to be happier. So showing the pupil those who are unhappy will prompt him to become more aware of others and more sensitive to them.
2. We must take pains to make our pupils aware of the fact that the sufferings of others can easily befall them as well. We do

not pity others unless we realize that the circumstances that led to their sufferings could do the same to us.

3.   We must fight the urge that we have to only pity those who think they need pity. That is, if someone has never had very much in his life, and does not realize that other people have it much better than he does, we are less apt to feel pity for him. But this is a great error, his suffering is the same: 'In a word, teach your pupil to love all men, even those who fail to appreciate him; act in such way that he is not a member of any class, but takes his place in all alike; speak in his hearing of the human race with tenderness, and even with pity, but never with scorn.'[19]

Cultivating pity according to these maxims allows us to extend self-love to others, which is what virtue really consists in for Rousseau. It gives us a sense of our own dependence on others, our vulnerability and the intrinsic badness of suffering no matter who it touches. From these realizations comes our sense of justice. We cease to constantly be pre-occupied with our own self interest:

The more care he bestows upon the happiness of others the wiser and better he is, and the fewer mistakes he will make between good and evil; but never allow any blind preference founded merely on personal predilection or unfair prejudice. Why should he harm one person to serve another? What does it matter to him who has the greater share of happiness, providing he promotes the happiness of all? Apart from self-interest this care for the general well-being is the first concern of the wise man, for each of us forms part of the human race and not part of any indi- vidual member of that race. To prevent pity from degenerating into weakness we must generalize it and extend it to mankind. Then we only yield to it when it is in accordance with justice, since justice is of all the virtues that which contributes most to the common good. Reason and self-love compel us to love man- kind even more than our neighbour, and to pity the wicked is to be very cruel to other men.[20]

We can see in the above passage how pity, a natural and amoral faculty in human beings, can, if cultivated properly, transform our sense of self-love into common moral notions of justice. We can summarize Rousseau's position as follows. We take an interest in ourselves; we look after our own well-being. This interest, this 'self-love', which manifests itself independently in the form of *amour de soi* or through our regard for others in the form of *amour-propre*, combined with pity, allows us to develop a genuine caring for others and for all of humanity. It allows us to arrive at basic moral precepts. The suffering of others is regrettable; people injuring other people is to be prevented whether we ourselves are one of the parties or not; and the golden rule: treat others as we want to be treated. From these precepts we arrive at the virtue justice.

Not only is Emile now old enough to learn about morality, but he is also ready to begin learning about religion. Unsurprisingly, Rousseau is extremely critical of teaching formal religion to children. He argues that when we teach them at a young age to memorize religious doctrine and definitions about God, they would simply have no idea what they were repeating and were likely to be turned off to the subject. Rousseau likely has the Roman Catholic Church in mind when he says, 'If I had to depict the most heart-breaking stupidity, I would paint a pedant teaching children the catechism; if I wanted to drive a child crazy I would set him to explain what he learned in his catechism.'[21] Remarks like these, combined with the philosophical claims Rousseau advocates in the *Profession of Faith of the Savoyard Vicar* that we shall see below, are primarily why Paris authorities immediately banned the *Emile*. Let us turn now to the *Profession of Faith*.

As stated above, the *Profession of Faith*, is presented as Rousseau's recalling the words that a priest once told him when he was a young man disillusioned about religion. What follows is a lengthy and complex philosophical account, which is significant because it represents Rousseau's most explicit and thorough discussion of several classic problems in philosophy. The priest explains that he came from humble beginnings, but that his parents wanted something better for him and so decided he should be a priest. Without really thinking carefully about the foundational beliefs of the Catholic Church, the young man went, completed his training, took his vows and became a priest. In the priest's words, he did not realize that in promising to obey these vows he did not realize that he had inadvertently 'promised not to be a man'. The vow of celibacy proved too much for him, and after breaking it, there was a great scandal and he was disgraced and sent to the country. He then reflected deeply on the nature of God, human beings and organized religion; these reflections are the substance of the treatise. I believe the most helpful way to think about the *Profession of Faith* is to conceive of it as a work in two main parts. The first part explains Rousseau's basic philosophical view of substance, free-will, the existence of God and morality. The second part draws conclusions from these claims about religion, namely the 'religion of nature'.

The priest explains that he began in a state of complete doubt, not unlike Descartes had famously done in his *Meditations*, and finds nothing in the work of the most brilliant philosophers of the time that is a matter of universal agreement among them. He therefore decides that he must develop a method of his own upon which to base his claims that is not subject to the same problems. The method he chooses is to follow what he calls the 'Inner Light of reason'; he also refers to the method as that of 'following his heart'. These phrases, I believe, are ways of advocating for a philosophy of common sense. Where I think this method differs from that of the other philosophers Rousseau criticizes (at least where I think Rousseau *intends* it to differ) is that he will not let basic premises lead him through logical implications to accept conclusions that seem, on the level of common sense, to be unreasonable. In the end the system he ends up with will be less robust than others, and will need to remain silent on many issues. But this is a sacrifice that he is perfectly willing to make: '[The Inner Light] will not lead me so far astray as others have done, or if it does, it will be my own fault, and I shall not go so far wrong if I follow my own illusions as if I trusted to their deceits'.[22] The other noteworthy aspect of the method is that it is concerned almost exclusively with contemplating philosophical issues only insofar as they have a practical application to one's life: 'The first thing I learned from these considerations was to restrict my inquiries to what directly concerned myself, to rest in profound ignorance of everything else, and not even to trouble myself to doubt anything beyond what I was required to know.'[23] At several points in the *Profession of Faith* the priest chastises philosophers for spending their time and energy debating very obscure and abstract questions, which ultimately, however they are answered, would not affect how we would live our lives. Far from having a practical relevance, these philosophers display a corrupted *amour-propre*, as they are far more interested in tearing down the ideas of other philosophers for the sake of fame than in actually ascertaining the truth: 'There is not one of them who, if he chanced to discover the difference between truth and falsehood, would not prefer his own lie to the truth which another had discovered'.[24]

Nevertheless, Rousseau is compelled to make several fairly ambitious philosophical claims. Whether or not he does this in a way that avoids the criticism he makes of other philosophers, however, is really for the reader to decide. Among the most significant claims, he argues that (1) He exists as does the external world; (2) God exists as a perfect being and the source of nature's design; (3) Human beings are free beings. Their movements are not reducible to material external causes; (4) Materialism (the view that all that exists is matter) is a false metaphysical doctrine and (5) Moral obligations and knowledge of virtue can be discerned by reason's examination of the natural order. Our limited space does not allow me to explain every detail of his argument for these claims, but I think it will be useful to treat each of them briefly. To help the reader keep track of this discussion, I have used the numbers I just assigned above, though Rousseau himself does not label them this way.

1. The first claim, knowledge of his own existence and the existence of the external world sounds very much like Descartes, who famously proclaimed 'I think therefore I am'. Our senses make us aware of our existence, and they continue to function without our willing them to do so. Thus, Rousseau concludes that there are objects outside himself, objects that affects his senses, which he calls matter. He therefore favours an empiricist rather than rationalist perspective. However, he does not bother to address what those bodies, which are collections of particles of matter, are like 'in themselves' as this is a speculative

philosophical question with no practical significance. Hence, 'the disputes of the idealists and realists have no meaning for me.'[25] Whatever the external world is 'in itself' (that is, what it is like apart from my own subjective experience of it), we observe that the objects in it, the bodies of matter, are in motion.

2. Reason can infer God's existence in two main ways according to Rousseau: from the nature of motion and from the design of the universe. Interestingly enough, both of these ways (at least versions of them) were used by previous thinkers to prove God's existence, most notably Aquinas who included these two among his famous 'Five Ways'.[26] As we noted above, Rousseau observes that matter is in motion, and that the motions he observes are always the result of some external cause. A classic example that philosophy professors like to use to illustrate this is a line of dominos that has fallen down. If we ask what caused the last domino in the line to fall, we would say that it was pushed down by the domino immediately behind it; and if we asked what caused *that* domino to fall, we would say it was the domino immediately behind the second to last domino, and so on and so on. But the line of dominos can not go on forever, there had to be a first domino, and that domino did not just move by itself. Something had to move it, someone had to push it, someone with a will who intended the dominos to fall. Of course this is not a perfect analogy, but I think it can help one understand where the argument is coming from. Rousseau states, 'The first causes of motion are not to be found in matter; matter receives and transmits motion, but does not produce it. The more I observe the action and reaction of the forces of nature playing on one another, the more I see that we must always go back from one effect to another, till we arrive at a first cause in some will.'[27] The argument for God as the 'First Mover', however, is less important than Rousseau's second argument for God's existence, God is necessary to explain the intention behind the natural order of the universe. The Inner Light tells us, Rousseau says through the priest, that there must be some perfect intelligence behind the order we see in the world around us. It cannot be, or at least it is extremely unlikely,

that the world around us was simply the result of chance. The odds of living beings coming into existence randomly are astronomical. This argument, given by Aquinas several hundred years before and based on final causality, was perhaps most famously advocated by William Paley with his watchmaker analogy as evidence of design. Even today, some contemporary philosophers of religion use a version of it that is known as the 'fine-tuning argument for God's existence', which is based in large part on modern physics. What is most important for Rousseau's version of the argument is that God has structured nature in a particular way, such that we as humans have a specific role to play. Therefore, understanding God as the intelligence behind nature's order will have great practical importance for Rousseau, as we shall see below in our discussion of (5). Rousseau understands God as a supremely perfect being, therefore he is perfectly intelligent, powerful and benevolent.

3. Rousseau's defence of human beings as creatures endowed with freedom echoes the claims made in the *Second Discourse*. There, we saw him equate freedom with the ability of a subject to go against instinct. Freedom combined with *perfectibility* is what allows human beings to leave nature, form society, and become moral creatures endowed with a developed sense of reason. In the *Emile*, Rousseau posits a similar notion of freedom, and gives more in the way of a philosophical defence of it against determinism (the view that all of our decisions are externally caused in such a way that we are unable, ever, to do otherwise). However, the defence he gives will likely not be very persuasive to those favouring determinism, as it is not so much an argument as it is an appeal to our common sense experience, an appeal once again to the Inner Light or voice of the heart. As we saw above in the preceding discussion of God and motion, Rousseau believes that matter cannot ultimately be its own source of motion and so a will is needed to explain it. The same is true of my own individual motions. I wish to move my arm and then I move it; the will causes the motion and is not, according to Rousseau, reducible to matter. But this raises a problem, one that has been around in philosophy for at least as

long as since Descartes posited the human soul as an immaterial substance, the so-called 'Mind/Body Problem'. In short, how can something immaterial 'push' on something material and make it move? The Mind/Body Problem has led many philosophers past and present to reject dualism (that we are composites of immaterial minds and material bodies), at least the Cartesian version of it. But Rousseau defends a dualistic view, arguing that if the will is somehow outside of the physical realm, which is causally determined, we can and in fact do act freely when we cause our own motion. The evidence for this is not a philosophical argument, but rather our own experience: 'You ask me again, how do I know that there are spontaneous [free] movements? I tell you, "I know it because I feel them." I want to move my arm and I move it without any other immediate cause of the movement but my own will. In vain would any one try to argue me out of this feeling, it is stronger than any proofs; you might as well try to convince me that I do not exist.'[28]

4.   The argument against materialism builds off Rousseau's view of freedom. Essentially, he is compelled to posit the existence of wills as immaterial entities because a materialist system is unable to explain human freedom, as well as where the universe came from (see the above discussion of God as the First Mover). It is not merely 'wishful thinking' that leads Rousseau to reject materialism, a mere wish that humans are free for example. He grants that issues like the Mind/Body problem are difficulties that he cannot solve, he is simply content to call them mysteries. But materialism is not without its own mysteries:

> The doctrine I have laid down is indeed obscure; but at least it suggests a meaning and there is nothing in it repugnant to reason or experience; can one say as much of materialism? Is it not plain that if motion is essential to matter it would be inseparable from it, it would always be present in it in the same degree, always present in every particle of matter, always the same in each particle of matter, it would not be capable of transmission, it could neither increase nor

diminish, nor could we ever conceive of matter at rest. When you tell me that motion is not essential to matter but necessary to it, you try to cheat me with words which would be easier to refute if there was a little more sense in them.[29]

The argument against materialism is an interesting example of Rousseau's method of following the Inner Light. We have two metaphysical theories: materialism, which states that all that exists is matter, and dualism, which states that there are material bodies as well as immaterial substances like the will. Both of these theories suffer from philosophical defects. Dualism has the Mind/Body problem, and materialism has the problem of explaining the relationship of motion to matter (see the above passage). So on what grounds can one choose one system over the other? According to the Inner Light, the heart, or common sense (whatever we call it), the view that my will is the source of spontaneous motion and my free actions, is so fundamental to my basic human experience that we should accept dualism rather than materialism.

5. Perhaps the most important philosophical claim that is made is the moral implication from the first four items we have just discussed. How should free beings designed by God exercise their freedom? Central to Rousseau's answer to this question is the faculty of 'Conscience', an innate principle of justice and virtue: 'Divine instinct, immortal voice from heaven; sure guide for a creature ignorant and finite indeed, yet intelligent and free; infallible judge of good and evil, making man like to God! In thee consists the excellence of man's nature and the morality of his actions.'[30] This divine instinct in us, conscience, is somewhat ambiguous, but in many ways it goes back to Rousseau's general idea of nature and indeed the basic educational programme in the *Emile*. When we stay close to nature, when we avoid vice, and when we cultivate ourselves properly, our perspective on the world and on each other will be in accord with nature, and God's, design. So we can then trust our inner voices. Rousseau does give us a bit more to go on than that, however. The clearest explanation of how to

understand morality is in Rousseau's discussion of virtue as a love or order:

> Wherever there is feeling and intelligence, there is some sort of moral order. The difference is this: the good man orders his life with regard to all men; the wicked orders it for self alone. The latter centres all things round himself; the other measures his radius and remains on the circumference. Thus his place depends on the common centre, which is God, and on all the concentric circles which are His creatures.[31]

The analogy of the circle is a helpful one, and we often use it to explain aspects of morality to people. We like to say 'You're not the center of the universe!' This essentially is what Rousseau is telling us, but he is doing it in a more nuanced and I think more literal kind of way. Gaining the moral, and natural perspective, comes from viewing oneself on the outside of the centre along with all others, looking to the centre which is God.

Why then, do we fail to take this perspective? Why is society plagued by vices? Rousseau's answer echoes another classic response to the problem of evil, the free will defence. It is not that God makes us bad; God makes all things good. Evil is the result of our using our freedom to go against our nature; against God: 'It is the abuse of our powers that makes us unhappy and wicked. Our cares, our sorrows, our sufferings are of our own making. Moral ills are undoubtedly the work of man . . .'[32] Evil is later defined by Rousseau as generally springing from disorder, in this case the order of nature; goodness by contrast is marked as accord with the natural order. Thus, justice, which seeks to restore and keep order, is inseparable from goodness.

Having laid down this basic philosophical framework, the priest proceeds to the second part of the *Profession of Faith*, the so-called 'Natural Religion', which is essentially a continuation of the moral perspective we just examined. We should also recall the earlier criticisms the priest has made regarding the lack of any legitimate need for revelation, as well as his scepticism about lengthy religious dogmas that do more to obscure the nature of God than to clarify it. The natural religion is therefore very general. Its basic tenets are that God is good and has a plan according to which we ought to live that we are free beings to live according to that plan or to go against it, and that the basic moral requirements are to view others' interests as being on par with our own. It can easily be observed that these claims are advocated by most if not all major world religions: 'God desires to be worshipped in spirit and in truth; this duty belongs to every religion, every country, every individual. As to the form of the worship, if order demands uniformity, that is only a matter of discipline and needs no revelation.'[33]

Rousseau bids us to think about the multitude of different religions that exist in the world. All of them seek to establish more specific grounds for the claims of natural religion. But the dogmas of the religions themselves only obscure the truths. Claims like these combined with the derogatory references made specifically to Roman Catholicism in the opening of the *Profession of Faith* were directly related to the *Emile*'s banning. For example, consider this statement of priest: 'I had been brought up in a church which decides everything and permits no doubts, so that having rejected one article of faith I was forced to reject the rest; as I could not accept absurd decisions, I was deprived of those which were not absurd. When I was told to believe everything, I could believe nothing, and I knew not where to stop.'[34] We now have the priest's answer to this dilemma. He can, in his heart though perhaps not publically, reject the Church's teaching on marriage and the celibacy of priests. But he can fully embrace its more general moral teachings that follow the example of Christ in loving God and one another. The latter teaching is fully recognizable as being in accord with the general truths of natural religion.

One particular concern Rousseau has with Christianity as it relates to other non-Christian religions has to do with eternal salvation. If salvation can only come through formally accepting Christ, as most Christian religions claim, then what can be said of those who are non-Christian; or of those who live in remote parts of the world who have never even heard of Christianity? Would these people all go to hell? 'If it were true that the gospel is preached throughout the world, what advantage would there be? The day

before the first missionary set foot in any country, no doubt some-
body died who could not hear him. Now tell me what shall we do
with him? If there were a single soul in the whole world, to whom
Jesus Christ had never preached, this objection would be as strong
for that man as for a quarter of the human race?"[35] I bring up this
example as I think it brings to light the way in which Rousseau says
religion ought to be regarded. To damn people who had no real
chance to save themselves would be unjust; and justice, as we have
seen is inseparable from God. If a particular religion makes a claim
like this about salvation, it ought to be rejected.

Considering the many religions in the world, the priest argues
that we can only really know whether one of them is 'true' to the
extent that we weigh its basic moral tenet against those of the natural religion. The specific dogmas of course cannot have the firm
grounding of reason, and there is no way to treat them objectively.
In fact, to evaluate all these religions against one another impartially,
to determine which of them is, 'the one true religion' would be
impossible. Each religious tradition is so incredibly rich that it
would take as many lifetimes as there are religions to *really* understand them without being biased to one's own tradition.

The priest does not advocate doing away with organized religion
however. On the contrary, he says that one should practice her own
religion (the religion in which she was brought up in or the religion
of the state) down to the letter, provided of course that this does not
require one to breach one of the duties of natural religion:

> As to those dogmas that have no effect upon action or morality,
> those dogmas about which so many men torment themselves, I
> give no heed to them. I regard all individual religions as so many
> wholesome institutions which prescribe a uniform method by
> which each country may do honour to God in public worship . . .
> I think them all good alike, when God is served in a fitting
> manner.[36]

In the end, the priest advocates a view to which I think many in our
own time are sympathetic. So long as natural religion is preserved,
any particular religion is as good as any other. No one religion has

the monopoly on the truth about God and revelation. Of course it goes without saying that such a view, while being inclusive in its own right, is in fact fundamentally incompatible with the claims of many of the most prevalent of the world religions, especially Christianity. As we shall see in the following chapter, a very similar account of civil religion is given in the *Social Contract*. The *Profession of Faith* as a work of metaphysics, moral philosophy and philosophy of religion remains one of Rousseau's most important writings. After its conclusion, Rousseau returns to the story of Emile.

Emile is now grown up for all intents and purposes, having reached his early twenties. To this point in his life, the tutor has used most of his efforts to keep Emile ignorant, lest he be corrupted by trying to learn about things that he was not yet ready for like morality, philosophy and religion. Now that he is ready to learn about these things, he is also ready to go out into society with his peers, though his fellow-men will not have had the benefit of the same education that Emile has had. And so a good deal of Emile's training has been to prepare him for their potentially dangerous influence. Emile has been brought up with a proper form of self-love, and will be able to preserve it, while at the same time being agreeable to those around him. Rousseau tells us that Emile will seem different to others, but in a very refreshing way, he will be like an 'agreeable foreigner ... everyone will like him without knowing why'.[37]

We can see by Rousseau's description of Emile in the latter part of Book Four exactly how his proper natural perspective determines his specific dealings with people. Since he is a 'savage' *made for society*, Emile is not at all anti-social; to the contrary, he is quite happy to deal with other people, even though they engage in actions have tastes that he does not agree with. In true keeping with his properly developed sense of self-love, Emile does not judge these people too harshly, nor does he have an inflated sense of self-worth about his moral superiority. Rather, he pities them; he knows that he cannot explain to them what is truly good as this would take years of the same education from which he benefited. He does not preach to them, nor does he cast judgement. He will not care much at all about public opinion, such as fashion trends or good etiquette, themes I see as similar to those Rousseau makes in the *First Discourse*. But what he does have is a genuine caring about other people, 'His heart is tender and sensitive, but he cares nothing for the weight of popular opinion, though he loves to give pleasure to others; so he will care little to be thought of as a person of importance.'[38]

The end of Book Four also begins the discussion of finding Emile a companion, a woman, which will ultimately be the main subject of the fifth and final book. The tutor and Emile discuss what an ideal woman would be like, and they even give her the name 'Sophy', though she is only imaginary at this point. The tutor will be careful to help Emile desire traits that are appropriate, and not surprisingly the women in Paris are not suitable for him. When he encounters women that may tempt him, the tutor will ask him, 'Would Sophy be that forward?' or 'Would Sophy act so shamelessly?' If Sophy is the perfect mate for Emile, she must have had just as good an education as he has had. Rousseau says she must be just as much the natural woman as Emile is the natural man. Book Five focuses in large part on the proper education of women, which we shall see is quite different than what Emile received.

Book Five

Book Five, like its predecessor is best understood in three main sections. The first is a philosophical account of female nature and the implications they have for the education of women. Next Rousseau describes the character of Sophy specifically. And finally, in the longest of the sections, Rousseau tells the story of Emile and Sophy's courtship, their engagement and ultimately their wedding and early years of marriage together. Rousseau's views of women, as they are given in Book Five, are not exactly progressive and the general response of feminists has not been positive at all. I think the reasons for this will be evident in the following discussion. Nevertheless, much of the educational process is aimed, as it was in Emile's education, at protecting Sophy (and presumably any young woman) from society's corruption. And so while I am sympathetic to claims of sexism against Rousseau, I think it would be a mistake to simply dismiss all he says outright. Therefore, in what follows, I have tried to give an impartial overview, so that the reader may decide for herself how we ought to view Book Five.

Rousseau's general view of men and women is that nature has made them complimentary to one another. There is, so to speak, human nature generally speaking, but there is also the male nature and the female nature. Each has certain strengths and certain weaknesses, and because they are complimentary, the strengths of one are oftentimes the weaknesses of the other. So the perfect man and the perfect woman will actually be quite different from one another. Rousseau, therefore, does not take himself to be arguing for the natural superiority of one sex (male) over the other. Nevertheless, his description of female nature in the opening of Book Five makes the following claims: 'the man should be strong and active; the woman should be weak and passive', 'woman is specially made for man's delight'[39] and 'Women do wrong to complain about the inequality of man-made laws; this inequality is not of man's making, or at any rate it is not a result of mere prejudice, but of reason'.[40] Rousseau tempers these claims about women being subservient to men, however, arguing that although they are the weaker and more passive sex, they actually have a great deal of control over men. Men are drawn to them and women can use their 'charms' (or perhaps manipulation is a more accurate term) to get what they want and to influence men. Part of the proper education of women, according to Rousseau, is to teach them to use these charms properly. But despite all of this, Rousseau is careful to indicate several times in Book Five that women are not to be treated as mere servants to men; that is not nature's way: 'On the contrary, nature means them to think, to will, to love, to cultivate their minds as well as their persons.'[41]

What are the specific aspects of female education? Like Emile's education, the education of a young girl must emphasize experience at the level for which the child is ready in her development. Recall the stories about the tutor and Emile when he was a boy. The tutor never taught lessons by lectures or with books but rather by structuring the environment in such a way that Emile would come to the lessons on his own. With women, Rousseau argues that this is perhaps even more important, as women by their nature are less apt than men when it comes to abstract reasoning. This is no more evident than in Rousseau's discussion of how to teach a young girl about religion. A woman's conduct, Rousseau argues, is controlled by public opinion, and so she should be taught religion as a matter of authority.

Furthermore, women are incapable of understanding the complex philosophical basis of religious beliefs. As such, women should dutifully follow the religion of their parents, the religion in which they were brought up. If the religion turns out to be false, the woman cannot be held blameworthy, as she is unable to deduce religious truths on her own. Interestingly, if one recalls the *Profession of Faith of the Savoyard Vicar* in Book Four, the priest says something quite similar. As long as the religion of one's upbringing is roughly in line with the basic morality of the religion of nature, one should practice it dutifully. For women, practicing the religion of their upbringing should be done for similar reasons, but even more so because of the women's philosophical ineptitude. What is far more important when it comes to religion are the practical implications. It is not so terribly important to come to definitive answers to questions about God's substance, or even about the sense in which Christ was 'God' anymore than deciding what day to celebrate a holiday. However, Rousseau says:

> . . . what does concern my fellow-creatures and myself alike is to know that there is indeed a judge of human fate, that we are all His children, that He bids us all be just, He bids us love one another, He bids us be kindly and merciful, He bids us keep our word with all men, even with our own enemies, and His; we must know that the apparent happiness of this world is naught, that there is another life to come, in which this Supreme Being will be the rewarder of the just and the judge of the unjust.[42]

The key to educating women is to strike the balance between making them merely servants to men, and making them attempt to usurp the role of men. As they are very practically minded and driven by emotions, according to Rousseau, female education is a cultivation of the attributes, a cultivation that would be wholly inappropriate for men.

We get a much clearer picture of what a properly educated woman looks like when Rousseau begins his discussion of the character of Sophy, who will ultimately marry Emile. Like Emile, there is nothing particularly exceptional about Sophy. She is not unusually intelligent, or beautiful; this is likely the case so as to emphasize that the educational programme does not require someone unusually gifted to be successful. Her favourite hobby is needlework, which Rousseau associates with the 'Feminine Arts'. There is a parallel between Sophy's needlework and Emile's learning carpentry; each needs to learn a craft, but the craft must be appropriate given their gender.

She is warm-hearted and merry, but she has a proper sense of modesty. Rousseau tells us that Sophy's parents have prepared her for marriage, but have not chosen a husband for her. They have trusted her to do it herself, and this is where Rousseau tells the story of Emile and Sophy, which comprises the end of Book Five and *Emile*. In keeping with the theme of structuring the pupil's environment throughout his life, we learn that Sophy has actually been discovered long ago. The tutor has known where she is all along. Recall that in Book Four he and Emile speak of what the ideal woman will be like and even give the imaginary woman the name 'Sophy'. Therefore, when Emile meets the actual Sophy, he is immediately captivated, wondering whether this might in fact be the perfect woman he has been imagining.

Having decided that Emile's future wife is not in Paris, he and the tutor leave for the country. They initially stay with a peasant there, who tells them of a family in the town that is better off than he and who is also very kind and generous. Emile is curious to meet these people, and so he and the tutor go to the house and given a warm welcome. They sit down to dinner with the owner of the house, his wife and their daughter who sits quietly and does not draw attention to herself. In fact, Emile is so taken with everything else around him that he barely notices her. But eventually, the mother refers to her by name, and as soon as Emile hears the word 'Sophy' he is immediately intrigued by her. Through the rest of the meal Emile cannot take his eyes off her, and after they leave he and the tutor stay up all night talking about her. After that first night, Emile and the tutor take up lodgings in the area and make frequent visits. Emile and Sophy grow closer, and eventually they become engaged.

In a somewhat strange turn, Emile in sense becomes a tutor to Sophy. She has not had the benefit of the kind of formal education he has had, and Emile is eager to debate and talk about philosophy with her. He eagerly tries to explain philosophy, as well as math and physics, though Rousseau reiterates his earlier claims about women's lack of ability in such subjects: 'Women are no strangers to the art of thinking, but they should only skim the surface of logic and metaphysics. Sophy understands readily, but she soon forgets. She makes progress in the moral sciences and aesthetics.'[43]

Following this discussion of Sophy's (somewhat limited) education, Rousseau turns to the subject of monogamy. He refers back to the *Second Discourse* when he says that the sexual desire that a man has for a woman can, once he has left the state of nature, manifest itself in the form of jealousy. Jealousy is a passion, one that can drive human beings to madness, and although it is not natural, it springs from the nature of a monogamous being. Rousseau defines monogamous creatures as those in which the sexual intercourse leads to some kind of moral bond. Though it is not entirely consistent with the pure state of nature as he describes it in the *Second Discourse*, he argues that the father was needed when children are first born since they are feeble and helpless for so long. Part of both Emile's and Sophy's education is to ensure that the natural bond they have will not degenerate into jealousy. For Emile, this is to ensure that his jealousy will not make him angry and suspicious, but rather timid and sensitive. For Sophy's part, her education will ensure that she does not become manipulative and deceitful, thus making it easier for Emile to control feelings that could become jealous passions.

Emile and Sophy have known each other for five months when, much to Emile's dismay, the tutor says he must leave Sophy. He does not mean that Emile must leave her for good, but rather that he should take a couple of years to travel, to see the world, and to make sure marrying her is the right thing to do. Emile is only twenty-two, and Sophy only eighteen; this is the time for love, but not yet the time for marriage according to the tutor. There is an additional reason that Emile must take this time however. He must learn how to be a citizen; the tutor asks, 'When you become a head of a family you will be come a citizen of your country. And what is a citizen of the state? What do you know about it? You have studied your duties as a man, but what do you know of the duties of a citizen?'[44] What follows is a brief account of the value of travel, of 'seeing the world' as it were, with a focus on Emile's observation of government and political rule. Here, Rousseau articulates several of the key themes of his political philosophy that are more fully discussed in the *Social Contract* and *Discourse on Political Economy*. Among these are ideas that were initially put forth in the *Second Discourse* namely that human beings are naturally free, and that legitimate power of the state can only exist when the sovereign power is in accordance with the collective common will of the citizens, which Rousseau terms the 'general will'. What Emile learns upon his travels is essentially the substance of Rousseau's criticisms of society in the *Second Discourse*; that nations are united by specious social contracts that the powerful enslave the poor through these contracts, and that the result of this arrangement is in large part the source of immorality and vice among human beings. After Emile learns these lessons, and his travel comes to an end, he realizes that his material possessions are not really important. In fact, they could even make him a slave if he does not keep the proper perspective. And so, he is willing to give them up, but the one thing he cannot give up is Sophy. His travels have only confirmed his love for her. Emile says to his tutor, 'But for my passions, I should be in my manhood independent as God himself, for I desire what is and I should never fight against fate. At least, there is only one chain, a chain which I shall ever wear, a chain of which I may be justly proud. Come then, give me my Sophy and I am free.'[45]

Emile ends with the wedding of Emile and Sophy, with the tutor imparting words of wisdom to both about how to remain in love. Then, a few months later, Emile happily announces to the tutor that he and Sophy are expecting a child of their own. Emile thanks the tutor and tells him to enjoy his 'well-earned leisure' as he will now have a pupil of his own to educate.

iii. EMILE AND SOPHY

It should be mentioned as we conclude this chapter that Rousseau wrote the beginning of a sequel to the *Emile* called 'Emile and Sophy'. The form of the sequel was a collection of letters from Emile to the tutor after he and Sophy had been married for several years. The work remains unfinished and what we have is the first letter and part of a second; the letters are written entirely as a novel as opposed to a philosophical treatise. What is most striking about *Emile and Sophy* is that the couple does not 'live happily ever after'. In fact, quite the opposite is the case. Basically, the story goes as follows. For some unknown reason, the tutor leaves and Emile and Sophy are on their own as a young married couple. They have a son and a daughter. But after both Sophy's parents and their daughter die, they decide to move out of the country and into Paris. Recall that in the *Emile*, Rousseau has nothing but contempt for the city, and so it is not surprising that things get worse for the couple when they move there. Emile and Sophy gradually grow further and further apart, with Emile blending more and more into the Parisian culture thus 'undoing' his natural education. Finally, Sophy reveals that she has had an affair and become pregnant with the other man's child. Emile takes a carpentry job to try to think through what to do. Ultimately he decides he must leave Paris in an effort to rediscover his true self. *Emile and Sophy* raises some very difficult questions. Most pressing is what we are to make of the plausibility of Rousseau's educational programme. Does the sad ending of Emile and Sophy's relationship mean the education was a failure? Does it mean that they simply should have avoided Paris, as no one can stay close to nature in such a corrupt society? Is it an indictment of female nature that Sophy was unable to remain faithful? We do not have solid answers to these questions unfortunately. The work itself is unfinished and Rousseau does not explicitly say what implications *Emile and Sophy* has for the original *Emile*. Nevertheless, the sequel shows Rousseau as true novelist, one who was compelled to continue the story of the characters he created.

iv. CONCLUSION

Emile is a book that is full of controversial claims. Rousseau's views on childrearing, religion and women are just a handful of examples. But perhaps those controversies, along with Rousseau's provocative and thoughtful arguments, are the reason *Emile* continues to be widely read and passionately discussed now more than 300 years after its publication. As was stated in the introduction to this chapter, *Emile*, though it is a vast work, is essentially an argument for one of Rousseau's most prevalent philosophical themes. Human beings are essentially good, or at the very least, uncorrupted. Working off this theme, *Emile* seeks to show how this goodness can be preserved, properly developed and enhanced. And all this can be done even in a corrupt, superficial and unjust society. Whether one agrees with the specifics of Rousseau's programme or not, the general aim is a noble one; one that can even give us hope for ourselves and our moral progress.

CHAPTER 5

POLITICAL PHILOSOPHY

i. INTRODUCTION

Rousseau's political philosophy is arguably the work for which he is the most famous. In this chapter, we will examine two of his major works on this subject: *The Discourse on Political Economy* and *The Social Contract*. The former was originally published as an entry in Diderot's *Encyclopédie* in 1755. The latter, which is generally considered to be Rousseau's most comprehensive work of political philosophy, came several years later in 1762; incidentally, this was the same year as the publication of *Emile*. And, like *Emile, The Social Contract* was immediately banned by Parisian authorities. There are certainly other works in addition to *The Discourse on Political Economy* and *The Social Contract* among Rousseau's writings that have significance for his political thought, but a thorough treatment of these two will, I believe, be sufficient so as to pull out the most important themes.

The best way to approach these two texts, and Rousseau's political thought generally, is to frame his ideas in the context of some of the more basic philosophical themes articulated in other works. And perhaps the best specific way to do this is to keep in mind the project of the *Discourse on the Origin of Inequality*, which we examined in Chapter 3. There, we saw a backward looking approach; using what Rousseau thinks is the most plausible conception of 'natural man', he then posits the historical events that must have occurred so as to arrive at 'civilized man'. We can recall that

Rousseau ultimately arrives at a very pessimistic view of civilized man, and of the civilized society in which civilized man lives. This civilized man of whom Rousseau speaks is of course the average contemporary citizen of his day, namely us. The existing social contract that binds us together arbitrarily grants power to some people rather than others, and maintains an unnatural and unjust inequality among its members. But we also saw Rousseau hint at the possibility of a different kind of social contract, one that is legitimate.

In *The Discourse on Political Economy* and *The Social Contract*, we get a picture of what such a society would look like. Thus, the primary goals of both texts are the same. In studying them, one is likely to notice a great deal of similarity between the two. Among the basic themes of the legitimate political regime that Rousseau articulates are (1) in line with nature, every citizen is equal to every other; (2) ruling power must ultimately rest with the people themselves; (3) the maintenance of the state cannot be preserved by the enforcement of specific rules; rather citizens must be of a certain kind of virtuous character to make it work; (4) the social contract preserves the freedom of each individual while she at the same time exists as a part of the whole. Keeping these general ideas in mind, let us now turn to *The Discourse on Political Economy*.

ii. THE DISCOURSE ON POLITICAL ECONOMY

Rousseau begins *The Discourse on Political Economy*, sometimes called the *Third Discourse* and which originally appeared as an entry in the *Encyclopédie*, by citing the origin of the word 'economy', which comes from the Greek words for 'house' and 'law'. In other words, to discuss economy is to focus on the appropriate governance of people. For the contemporary reader, it maybe helpful to keep this in mind as it is not the way we typically understand the word economy today. Rousseau is not giving a discourse that pertains only to wealth and distribution of goods. The scope is far more general; it is a work of political philosophy, specifically aimed at determining the first principles of legitimate government, the basic duties of a government to its citizens, and of citizens to each other.

There are two types of economy, two 'houses' so to speak. The first is the household, the private family, which Rousseau terms the *domestic economy*. *Political Economy* is concerned with the second type of house, the public family, more commonly referred to as the state. Perhaps because prominent authors had argued otherwise, a large portion of the *Third Discourse* seeks to demonstrate the vast differences between these two types of economy. The aims, methods and goals of a magistrate, as well as his or her relationship with the citizens do not parallel those of a father and his relationship to his wife and children. Let us investigate a few of these differences.

The first difference results from a practical problem, the fact that a state is much larger than a private family. A father can 'see all', or at the very least he can know each of his family members intimately and have a genuine sense of what is going on with each of them. It would be impossible for a magistrate to have such a perspective on his people. Even a small state is no exception. Imagine a small town of a few thousand people. A mayor could never know each of the town's citizens as well as a father knows his family members. Human beings simply do not have the capacity to have that many close relationships. Thus, even if *in principle*, leaders of political economies should govern in the same way that fathers govern households, it would be practically impossible to put such a method into practice. Some type of second best approach would need to be discovered for magistrates.

Rousseau goes further than this however. He argues that the differences between how a father should rule as compared with a magistrate are not merely practical. They do in fact differ in principle. That is to say, even if a magistrate *were* able to 'see all', to know each citizen as well as the father knows his family members, he should nevertheless rule in a different way. Rousseau states, 'Although the functions of the father and the chief magistrate should lead to the same goal, their paths are so different, their duties and rights so distinct, that one cannot confuse them without forming false ideas about the fundamental laws of society and without falling into errors fatal to the human race'.[1] Interestingly and even a bit surprisingly, one of the differences between father and magistrate is that the former can follow the 'voice of nature' whereas the latter cannot. Why is this surprising? Because if we recall other works, particularly the *Second Discourse* and *Emile*, Rousseau states repeatedly that we ought to in a sense return to nature, and that nature makes all things good. Why then, when it comes to political rule, does Rousseau caution against nature rather than embrace it, as he does for the rule of the household? There are several reasons.

First, the father has a natural impulse to love his children and to take care of them; and they in turn have an impulse to love and respect him. The father has a natural right of property within the household since the children are born into it and raised by him. In political terms, therefore, the relationship between the ruler and the ruled is based in nature when it comes to the household. By contrast, in a state, there is no such basis. To see where Rousseau is coming from here, simply imagine five grown adults of relatively the same health, strength and intelligence. Suppose one of these five people is to have a position of power over the others. How might we settle which of them should rule? We would probably want to base our decision on which of them would do the best job. We would want to know if any of them had any prior ruling experience, which had the best ideas for how she would rule, which was the most organized, etc. But on the surface, it would not be the case that one of them was entitled by nature to rule over the others. And although this claim probably seems obviously true to us, it varies from the tradition of Aristotle that enlightenment thinkers were challenging during Rousseau's time.

According to Aristotle, some people were naturally disposed to rule while others were naturally disposed to *be* ruled.[2] Often, this is referred to as Aristotle's defence of 'natural slavery'. Rousseau and others in the enlightenment period argued instead for the natural equality of human beings (once again, recall the central claims of the *Second Discourse*). This idea, now almost universally accepted in most of Western culture, does come with a problem, however. Since one person's authority over another is not based in nature, it must instead be based on some other factor/s. Such factors would include a good deal of luck such as where one was born, the circumstances of her upbringing, etc. But this would mean that all those in power have their power arbitrarily, and therefore certain safeguards need to be taken to ensure that the state is run justly.

Rousseau articulates four distinct reasons that nature dictates the father as the ruler of the household. None of these four, he argues, corresponds to the ruler of the state, the magistrate. In summary they are: (1) the government, in the case of the household this consists of the mother and the father, must be unified. If there is a disagreement between them, one (the mother, – see item 2), must defer to the other (the father) so as to present an authoritative voice to the other members of the household; (2) the husband/father should be the ruler of the household. This echoes what we have just seen in item (1), but here Rousseau justifies the claim in an interesting way. He claims that because women must endure the trauma of childbirth, they are left incapacitated for brief periods. Even though this may be only a slight difference between men and women, it is enough to tilt the balance of power to the husband. Given the need for a unified and authoritative voice, one of the two must have power over the other. Perhaps out of his own paranoia and his fear of women being unfaithful, Rousseau curiously adds that an additional reason that husbands should be able to control the conduct of their wives is to keep them faithful. This ensures that he is not forced to acknowledge and raise illegitimate children in his household (3). Children should obey their father. Initially they do this because they have no choice; when they are small, they depend on their father (and mother) to survive. So they must obey. When they grow older, children obey their father out of a sense of gratitude for raising them (4). The other members of the household, the servants, owe obedience to the father/husband for their livelihood as is the case in any employer/employee relationship. However, the servants can break ties with him if the relationship ever becomes inappropriate (that is exploitative).

There is nothing like these aforementioned four principles in the state according to Rousseau. There are no natural ties between the magistrate and the people. The ruler has no reason to love the people as the father loves his children; on the contrary, rulers often look after their own interests which commonly clash with those of the people. This is one of the few places in Rousseau's work in which there is an explicit warning *against* looking to nature:

> In fact, if nature's voice is the best advice a father can listen to in fulfilling his duties, it is, for the magistrate, nothing but a false guide which constantly works to divert him from fulfilling his own, and which sooner or later leads to his downfall or to that of the state, unless he is restrained by the most sublime virtue. The only precaution necessary for the father of a family is to protect himself from depravity and to prevent his own natural inclinations from becoming corrupted, but these are the very inclinations that corrupt the magistrate.[3]

If the private family, and hence the voice of nature, is insufficient for determining the proper way for a state to be governed, Rousseau must then give some alternative. What follows is the articulation of perhaps the most important element in his political philosophy that of the 'General Will'.

To introduce the concept of the general will, Rousseau begins with an analogy that was commonly used by other political philosophers at the time; Hobbes, for example, uses it in the *Leviathan*.[4] Rousseau compares the state, the political body, to an individual physical body. He identifies the functions of various parts of the state with those of organs and other body parts:

> The sovereign power represents the head: the laws and customs are the brain, the center of the nervous system and seat of the understanding, the will, and the senses, of which the judges and magistrates are the organs; commerce, industry, and agriculture are the mouth and stomach which prepare the common subsistence; public finances are the blood that a wise *economy*, performing the functions of the heart, sends back to distribute nourishment and life throughout the body; the citizens are the body and members which make the machine move, live, and work, and which cannot be injured in any way without a painful sensation being transmitted right to the brain, if the animal is in a state of good health.[5]

The analogy is supposed to show that the state is a unified whole. Each person has many different parts, a brain, a heart, blood, limbs, etc. But each is one person, one individual; in the same way, the state is one individual despite the fact that it too has many parts (the magistrate, public finance, the citizens, etc.). All of the individual parts of the body perform specific functions of course, but without conceiving of those functions within the context of a unified and organized whole, the particular functions themselves make no sense. When there is no unity, when the organization is lost, we no longer have a person anymore properly speaking. This, essentially, is the difference between a living human being and a human corpse. The same is true of the state according to Rousseau, when the formal unity ceases, the state is dissolved.

Continuing with the analogy, Rousseau explains that like individual persons, states are 'moral beings'; therefore, just as each individual has a will, so does the state. Each individual has a conception of herself *as herself*, and as a collection of her various parts. When one makes decisions, she does so with an eye toward what will be best for her overall as a whole, but she also looks at the well-being of each part. At first glance this might seem a bit puzzling, maybe even contradictory. How can one look after his welfare both as a whole *and* to each individual part? To understand this, we might elaborate on Rousseau's analogy between the state and the individual, and consider how one person regards herself in both these ways.

Suppose that I am interested in improving my health. I might begin working out several times a week. I would want to cultivate all of my different muscles with various different kinds of exercises. I would try to eat a balanced diet, get plenty of rest and so forth. In doing all these things, it seems as though I can regard myself as a one unified whole, and talk about 'my health' generally. But I can also view myself as a collection of individual parts, and for each of these parts, I can consider its particular welfare. I can think about my upper body, my lower body, my cholesterol levels, my body fat, my cardiovascular system and so on. I want each of these parts to function well, and I look at each of them individually. When I have the proper perspective, there is a great harmony between the welfare of each of the parts and the welfare of myself as a whole. We might even say that the welfare of the whole is the collective welfare of each of the parts. And most of the time, under normal circumstances, we can preserve this harmony. This is the essence of the general will, which Rousseau states as the first principle of public economy.

To sacrifice the welfare of one of the parts supposedly for the health of the other would be wrong. For example, suppose that I want to be extremely strong physically, so I begin taking steroids to build muscle mass. Now it might be that I get stronger, but steroid abuse can also cause heart disease, liver damage and various other dangerous side-effects. So if I ignore the welfare of the other parts and sacrifice them to focus too much on one of the others, I go against the general will.

However, this is not to say that the general will *never* proscribes sacrificing one part of the sake of the whole. Suppose that one of my legs becomes terribly infected, and to keep the infection from spreading, the doctors tell me they must amputate it. Obviously, the leg will have no chance of surviving the amputation, but in such a desperate situation, the welfare of the whole necessitates that I sacrifice this part. But where do we draw the line between cases like steroid abuse and cases like amputation when it comes to discerning the general will when it comes to the state; when the parts in question are the magistrates, the finances, trade and commerce, and most crucially, the various groups of citizens themselves? This is one of the fundamental questions Rousseau's political philosophy attempts to answer. First and foremost, the general will is to be contrasted with 'particular wills'. And here is where the analogy between the state and the individual body breaks down. Though my individual body parts and organs have specific functions, they do not have wills of their own. My arm never consciously tries to do one thing at the expense of my liver for example. But in a state, which as we have seen is one unified whole with a general will, there are also smaller groups, which are themselves composed of even smaller groups, and so on all the way down to the level of individual citizens. Each individual and each subordinate group does have a will of its own. The general will looks always to the common good, but the particular good only looks to the good of its particular faction or individual. When I act from my particular will at the expense of the general will, I am being a bad citizen. For example, if I am a member of a corporation, and I vote for political candidates and public policy based on what will benefit the corporation rather than what is for the overall common good, I am being directed by my particular will and not the general. Thus, Rousseau states, 'A certain person may be a devout priest, or a brave soldier, or a zealous professional, and yet a bad citizen'.[6] Since individuals and smaller groups are all subordinate to the largest group, the state, justice requires that the general will be followed rather than any particular will. To ensure that justice is served, Rousseau articulates three maxims to follow. His discussion of these maxims comprises the rest of the *Third Discourse*.

The first maxim, and according to Rousseau the most important, is essentially a restatement of preceding account of the general will, namely that a good government must follow the general will in all things. Most of Rousseau's discussion of the first and second maxims is not an argument for this claim *per se*, but rather an explanation of how to deal with the problem just mentioned, namely how we might distinguish between the general will and the particular will/s. He states:

This distinction is always extremely difficult to make, and only the most sublime virtue is capable of shedding light on it. Since it is necessary to be free in order to will, another difficulty no less great is to insure both public liberty and governmental authority. Inquire into the motives that have brought men, united by their mutual needs in the great society, to unite themselves more closely by means of civil societies, and you will find no other motive than that of insuring the property, and liberty of each member through the protection of all. But how can men be forced to defend the liberty of any one among them without infringing on the liberty of others? And how can public needs be met without doing some damage to the private property of those who are forced to contribute to them?[7]

The difficulty that Rousseau articulates in this passage seemingly takes the form of a paradox: to will any action one must be free, but to have my particular will constrained by an outside force is to *not* be free. It would be very strange indeed if a just society was one in which people were no longer free beings. Certainly Rousseau wants to advocate just the opposite that a legitimately governed state is one in which each citizen's freedom is protected and can even flourish. The difficulty, the seeming paradox, is solved by the law according to Rousseau. The law is described in almost poetic terms, as the miracle that provides justice and equality, and even as the 'celestial voice' that dictates public reason to the citizens. At first glance, this may seem a bit puzzling. We normally do not think of the law this way at all. Rather, in our everyday lives, we often simply think of the law as those rules passed down by government that we must obey lest we be punished for breaking them. It is not as though we do not appreciate the importance of the law, or that we do not feel compelled to respect it, but we typically do not think of the law as that which makes us free. And we can easily come up with historical examples of laws that were violations of justice such as segregation laws or laws discriminating against Jewish people in Nazi Germany. So, Rousseau obviously has something different in mind here, he does not mean to say that any rule handed down by a government as a 'law' necessarily protects freedom and justice.

Rousseau is not terribly specific about what kinds of laws should be instituted in this section, but he does tell us several general things about them. First, the laws must conform to the general will; this may seem a bit circular seeing as how the maxim itself is to follow the general will. But we should remember that the general will is always for the good of the whole, and so to follow it in law-making will be in large part an effort at being impartial. No one individual or subordinate group of citizens should be given preference over the rest. The examples of unjust laws that I cited previously, segregation laws and the laws of the Nazis, fail for this reason (though of course they fail for many other reasons too). Far from being impartial, they arbitrarily make on group of citizens superior to another.

Along the same lines, Rousseau states that the magistrates themselves must obey the law, so as to show that no one is above the law. Again this ensures impartiality, and preserves the natural equality among human beings. And finally, the laws must be loved by the citizens. We shall see below in the second maxim that Rousseau defines virtue as the harmony of particular wills with the general. But virtue cannot be coercive. We cannot ensure that law will protect freedom if we enforce it by merely instilling a fear of terrible punishment. If we did, people will not obey because they celebrate the common good, and thus obey it *freely*. Rather they will obey it to avoid punishment, a motive which is tied to their individual particular wills. Therefore, to follow the general will in all things, we first must establish and then revere the law.

The second maxim re-emphasizes the importance of conforming particular wills to the general so as to ensure that the general will can be carried out in all things as per the first maxim. Rousseau then defines virtue itself as this conformity, and so says another way of stating the second maxim is to 'let virtue reign'. Virtue, for Rousseau, is a difficult concept to grasp. He speaks of it often and in many different texts. To gain an appropriate understanding of it, one must pay careful attention to the context in which he uses the term. For example, in *Emile* and *First Discourse*, Rousseau often describes the rejection of public opinion and the condemnation of one's society as virtuous. In the *Third Discourse*, by contrast, virtue is associated with submitting one's particular will to the general and almost submitting one's individuality to the state. Though it may seem as if Rousseau is using the term virtue in a contradictory manner, I think instead we ought to remember that in *Emile* and *First Discourse*, Rousseau is considering how to conduct oneself in an unjust regime. In the *Third Discourse*, he is considering the ideal state. Thus, what it means to be virtuous for a given individual with respect to how she conducts herself within her society will be determined to a large extent by how just that state is.

In his discussion of the second maxim, Rousseau offers several specific suggestions for *how* we might ensure that we 'make virtue reign'. The first, however, is an indication of what will not work in this respect. We can never ensure that people will conform their particular wills to the general by implementing rules. One might recall a similar notion in *Emile*, when Rousseau argues that children cannot be taught to be good by forcing them. That will only make them do what is right for fear of punishment. In a state, this same phenomenon will occur among the citizens. People will merely look for loopholes in the rules that they might use to exploit for their own gain at the expense of the state. Rousseau states, 'The worst of all abuses is to appear to obey the laws, while, in truth, breaking them with safety'.[8] So virtue cannot be achieved by coercion, but instead must be a matter of the heart. To be virtuous is to have a certain kind of character, in this case an endearing love for the homeland, the state in which one lives. Like any state of character, virtue is acquired by habit. To instil a love of the state, a love of one's duty, citizens must be brought up from the very beginning to see the benefits that their homeland provides for them.

Two of these benefits stand above the rest for Rousseau: equality and liberty. When there are gross inequalities among groups of citizens, when some are very rich and others are very poor, it is only natural that the poor will come to feel disillusioned and even resentful of the state. Equality, though, like virtue itself cannot be forced upon people. So Rousseau does not say we should simply take away from those with much and give to those with little, but rather that we should put mechanisms in place to prevent those inequalities from coming to be in the first place. Though it risks circularity, he argues that when people are virtuous, they will not allow such inequalities because they will recognize the conflict of them with the general will.

The discussion of liberty that Rousseau offers similarly returns to the notion of virtue itself. One cannot have liberty without having virtue, and one cannot have virtue without having true citizens. Again, one might pose the charge of circularity here, and point out that Rousseau's answer to the question of how to make true citizens is to make people virtuous. But I would stop short of such a criticism, primarily because of what Rousseau describes following these remarks. He returns to the theme of education, stating:

> If, for example, they [the citizens] are trained early enough never to consider their own persons except in terms of their relations with the body of the state, and not to perceive of their own

existence, so to speak, except as a part of that of the state, they may finally succeed in identifying themselves in some way with this greater whole, in feeling themselves members of the homeland, in loving it with that exquisite sentiment which every isolated man feels only for himself, in perpetually lifting up their souls toward this great objective, and thus transforming into a sublime virtue that dangerous disposition from which all our vices arise.[9]

And so once again we come to the importance of instilling morality, or at least protecting against the corruption of morality, from the very beginning. If we teach citizens from their birth that they are a part of something bigger, and if they regard themselves as citizens first and individuals second, we will ensure that they will be virtuous. Problems of keeping equality and of just law-making will then take care of themselves for the most part. But without virtue, these same problems become insurmountable.

The third and final maxim states that the basic needs of the people must be satisfied. The maxim works on the basic idea that citizens will not, and perhaps even *cannot*, love the state if they do not have these needs met. Rousseau runs through several topics that relate to this notion, among them property rights, taxation and equal protection under the law.

With the attacks that Rousseau levels against the notion of private property in other works, especially the *Second Discourse*, I believe there is a danger in mistakenly attributing to him the view that property is necessarily evil and corrupting. This has led many to accuse Rousseau of being a communist in the worst sense of the term. Of course property and disputes over it can and have led to a great deal of misery among people. However, Rousseau says in the *Third Discourse* that property rights are the most sacred and claims that they lie at the very foundation of civil society. So in describing the ideal state, he does not argue for the elimination of private property altogether. To the contrary, most of the discussion is in defence of inheritance laws that allow people to pass their property on to their surviving relatives after death.

With respect to taxation, Rousseau argues that a group of leaders is needed to administer taxes to the people and to control the public domain. The need for this is a practical one, as 'civil society is always too large in number to be governed by all the members'.[10] Taxes must be governed by necessity and kept meticulously; money set aside for one purpose should almost never be redirected to another. Rousseau goes so far as to call this theft. Most importantly, taxes should not be used to fix problems, but rather to prevent them from occurring in the first place. In this spirit, Rousseau mentions his homeland of Geneva, praising it for establishing reserve granaries to pre-emptively guard against famine. Citizens should be taxed according to what they have, and not 'by the head'. He states, '. . . anyone who has ten times more wealth than another should pay ten times more than the poorer one . . . Anyone who has only the bare necessities should pay nothing at all'.[11]

And finally, citizens need basic protection. Here, once again, Rousseau's main concern is to point out that the quality of one's protection should not be affected by wealth:

> A third relationship that is never taken into account, although it should always be considered first of all, is that of the benefits everyone derives from the social confederation, which provides a powerful protection for the immense possessions of the rich and scarcely allows a poor wretch to enjoy the cottage he has built with his own two hands.[12]

Here, Rousseau describes a phenomenon that many of us find disturbing in current day society. Many of us are suspicious that those with wealth are able to get away with more while those who are poor are not. Furthermore, if a rich person is wronged, the authorities go to great lengths to serve justice. By contrast, we fear that when the poor are wronged, they are given relatively little attention by the police and legal authorities. In the worst cases, their complaints are met with suspicion that the victims themselves are guilty of wrongdoing! This injustice cannot be tolerated according to Rousseau.

Thus, concludes *The Discourse on Political Economy*. The prevailing theme, I believe, is that the problems that plague political society can only be solved by having citizens of a certain kind of character, a true love for the homeland and a dedication to the general will. These points will be fundamental in *The Social Contract* as well, which we will examine in the following section.

iii. THE SOCIAL CONTRACT

The Social Contract is comprised of four books, each of which is subsequently divided into several chapters. The specific chapters are relatively short and to discuss each of them individually would I believe make my discussion rather cumbersome. Therefore, I have divided my account of *The Social Contract* into four parts, each corresponding to a book of the text. Because Rousseau's central goal in *The Social Contract*, to articulate the creation and mainten-ance of a legitimate political regime, parallels that of *The Discourse on Political Economy*, there are many similarities between the two works. Rather than repeat earlier discussions, I have made refer-ences back to the *Third Discourse* when necessary. However, I believe that *The Social Contract* is in many ways an expansion of the central arguments made in *Third Discourse*. Rousseau spells out seemingly ambiguous concepts in more detail, and gives more specific accounts of some of the political strategies he proposes. My primary goal in what follows, therefore, is to elucidate these points and show how they further support the main tenets of Rousseau's political philosophy.

Book One

Book One opens with Rousseau's stated goal of defining the ideal political regime, and follows in the book's first chapter with one of his most famous declarations: 'Man is born free, and everywhere he is in chains'.[13] What does Rousseau mean by this? The answer, I think, is fairly obvious to one who is familiar with Rousseau's other works, especially the *Second Discourse, Emile*. Recall in the former that Rousseau sees the social contract under which we currently operate as illegitimate. It is this same society whose dan-gerous influences pose the greatest threat to Emile's education. So,

Rousseau's claim is a descriptive one; it is *we* who are in chains. The vision of *The Social Contract* provides a way to break the chains while preserving the institution of civil society.

Following the *Third Discourse*, Rousseau cites the private family as the original form of civil society, and the seeming parallel between the father and the magistrate. He points to the fact that the father is in a sense naturally superior to the other family members, and is thus a natural ruler. However, Rousseau argues against extending this claim to human beings generally, which is similar to Aristotle's argument for natural slavery. We saw this above in the discussion of the *Third Discourse*. He similarly argues against Grotius, whom he sees as advocating that a hundred or so men rule the rest of the human race. And finally he argues against Hobbes, who he claims has placed the sovereign ruler in a position of ruling superiority over the people. Ironically, Hobbes is in fundamental agreement with Rousseau about the natural equality of human beings.

The primary mistake that Aristotle, Grotius and Hobbes all make, according to Rousseau, is to confuse the question of what *is* with the question of what *ought to be*. If we examine the world around us, we do see just the kinds of inequalities that these authors describe. This mistake can also lead us to another mistaken notion, one that many of us find compelling on some level: 'Might Makes Right'. We may be inclined to think that the law of a given society is whatever rules the government lays down that we are compelled to follow. Whoever has the power to enforce the rules decides what is right and wrong. Rousseau rejects this however. While it may be an apt description, it fails to establish anything other than obedience out of fear. 'Might Makes Right' can never give anyone a genuine sense of duty. It is not sufficient so as to give me a real moral obligation. In a clever example Rousseau states, 'If a thief surprises me in a corner of the woods, I am forced to give him my purse, but am I, in conscience, obligated to give it to him when I could hide it?' The laws of the state are the same way. If they are unjust like the robber in the woods, I may follow them out of prudence, but I certainly cannot be said to be obligated.

From here, Rousseau moves to a discussion of the 'Social Pact' (which is the title of Book One Chapter 6) and returns to the notion of the state of nature. His discussion of the beginnings of society here, however, varies with the story he tells in the *Second Discourse*. There, we saw that Rousseau describes the process as very slow and almost unintentional; the people entering into society do not do so intentionally or consciously. In *The Social Contract*, Rousseau represents the move from nature to civil society as a much more deliberate process. He simply says that men have 'reached the point at which the obstacles to their preservation in the state of nature have a resistance greater than the forces each individual can us to maintain himself in that state'.[14] The language here seems very similar to Hobbes. Basically, human beings reach a point at which their self-preservation is best maintained by joining together with others. But where Rousseau differs from Hobbes is in the way that each of the citizens now views herself once she has entered into civil society. For Hobbes, they remain individualistic and this is precisely why the sovereign must keep them in line by terror. This presents civil war. For Rousseau, there is a kind of transformation that takes place in the way each person regards herself. This is a crucial point, and helps Rousseau to deal with what he takes to be a fundamental difficulty in explaining how liberty can be preserved in a state. Above we saw him discuss this problem at length in the *Third Discourse*. Instead of regarding ourselves as individuals, we regard ourselves first and foremost as parts of a whole. The crucial element that a social pact needs for this to occur is equality among the parts. Each person gives herself entirely, so no one is any more or any less a part of the whole than anyone else. Rousseau sums it up this way in the text: 'Each of us puts his person and all his power in common under the supreme control of the general will, and, as a body, we receive each member as an indivisible part of the whole'.[15]

The mention of the general will, which we have already seen is one of the most important themes in Rousseau's political thought, leads to the notion of sovereignty. The sovereignty is not a separate ruler that looks down on the people. Rather, the people themselves as a collective entity are their own sovereign. Just as we saw in the *Third Discourse*, having a legitimate state with legitimate sovereignty requires that the citizens regard themselves in the right way.

Sovereignty will be discussed further in Book II where Rousseau claims that it is nothing more than the exercise of the general will.

In our discussion of the *Second Discourse*, we saw that Rousseau praised many aspects of the state of nature. But he criticized much about modern day society. We saw an even more robust set of such criticism in *Emile*. In both of these texts, however, we saw Rousseau pointing to the ideal regime. In such a state, human beings would not merely be good in the amoral sense that they are not wicked as they are in the state of nature. They would be morally good, actually virtuous. It is this ideal state, and not the currently existing one, that Rousseau is referring to when he says:

> The passage from the state of nature to the civil state produces a most remarkable change in man, by substituting justice for instinct in his conduct, and giving his actions the morality they previously lacked. Only when the voice of duty succeeds physical impulse and right succeeds appetite does man, who had until then considered only himself, find himself compelled to act on different principles and to consult his reason before listening to his inclinations.[16]

Here once again, we see Rousseau articulating the theme of gaining liberty by giving up individual freedom.

The final chapter of Book I, Chapter 9, deals primarily with the notion of property, specifically land. And here, we get a somewhat clearer picture of Rousseau's view than we saw in the *Third Discourse*. In short, his position is that while the right of first occupancy does and should apply to private individuals and their property (those who get to the land first, take only as much as they need, and acquire it by labour), the community has an overriding right to that property should there be a legitimate public need for it arise. This may seem unjust. One might ask, 'What right has the government to take *my* property?' But according to Rousseau, the only reason one has property in the first place is because of the institution of civil society. Landowners owe the very fact of having land to the state, and so their right to the land is subordinate to the rights of the state.

Book Two

Book Two expands on two crucial themes that Rousseau introduces in Book One, namely those of the general will and sovereignty. To call these two *different* notions may be a bit misleading however. Sovereignty, or legitimate ruling, is nothing more than the exercise of the general will. This exercise is always, by definition, aimed at the common good of the society. Thus, the two concepts are intimately intertwined. In the opening of Book Two, Rousseau marks two characteristics of sovereignty. It is both 'inalienable' and 'indivisible'.

To say that sovereignty is inalienable is to say that it cannot be transferred from one party to another, nor can it be discarded or rejected. The meaning of this may not be immediately clear, as there are many other instances in which the exercise of a ruling power is not inalienable. Perhaps an example will elucidate this point. Suppose that I am the coach of a sports team. In a sense, I exercise my rule over the team members by performing the normal duties of coaching. But clearly this power can be transferred, and I could even transfer it myself. I may resign and name one of my assistant coaches as the new head coach. We could also imagine my power to simply be rejected. Suppose that the players on my team think I am doing a poor job and, in what they take to be the best interest of the team, they simply stop obeying the rules I set out for them. But true sovereignty can never be transferred or rejected in this manner. Sovereignty is a collective entity; there are certainly those in a society who are charged with being its mouthpiece (in Book Three Rousseau will call them the 'government'), but they themselves are not the sovereign. Even in my coaching example, I used the phrase 'the best interest of the team'. Whatever is in the best interest is the general will of the team, collectively understood as a unified whole entity. So, if I am making poor coaching decisions, then I myself am violating the general will and therefore not exercising it. Hence for the players to reject me is not a rejection of the sovereign.

The inalienable nature of the sovereign relates to its *indivisibility* as well. The general will is collective, and each citizen constitutes an equal part. But it is also unified; it speaks in only one voice. Clearly there are times in any group in which the various group's members disagree with one another. Even if the members in question are those charged with making decisions on behalf of it, the conflict is between particular wills. Rousseau is careful to make this point because he anticipates a possible objection to sovereignty's indivisibility. We may think that the sovereignty is divided, citing the separation of powers in many governments. On such a view, sovereignty would only be indivisible in an absolute monarchy. For example, in the United States, only congress can declare war. However, other branches of government have powers that congress does not have. One may be inclined to say that the exercises of all the various powers are acts of sovereignty. So sovereignty is divided among the various government branches. But this is misleading according to Rousseau. He argues that 'This error results from not having formulated an accurate notion of sovereign authority, and from having taken for parts of that authority what were only emanations of it'.[17]

Since the general will, by definition, is always for the common good, it can never be in error. The general will is never 'wrong'. But we should not confuse this with thinking that government officials can never make a mistake. In practical application, those charged with trying to put the general will into practice can indeed make mistakes. In these cases, it is not that the general will has gone wrong, but rather that either intentionally or unintentionally the government officials have substituted some private will for the general will and exercised it instead. Because each citizen is an equal part of the social pact, representing the whole of the state, legitimate expressions of the general will benefit all members equally.

Rousseau also takes on the interesting question of the possible limits to sovereign power. Can the general will of a state ever ask one of its citizens to make *too* great a sacrifice? Once again, there is a difference between what the general will say conceptually and what those charged with exercising may mistakenly take it to be saying. Not surprisingly, the general would not and in fact *could not* ask more of a citizen than that citizen was obligated to give. We have seen similar reasoning throughout Rousseau's discussion of the general will. Such questions essentially amount to asking, 'Can the right thing to do ever be wrong?' The answer is of course 'no'. However, with regard to the possibility of the general will erring, Rousseau does offer a suggestion so as to distinguish when state actions go beyond the general will and only express the particular will of an individual or faction. He says:

> A citizen owes to the state all the services he can render, as soon as the sovereign asks for them, but the sovereign, on the other hand, cannot impose on the subjects any restrains that are useless to the community, nor can it even want to do so, for, under the law of reason just as under the law of nature, nothing is done without a cause.[18]

Discussions like the preceding inevitably lead us to a crucial question for Rousseau's political philosophy. If we accept the general will in principle as that which ought to guide the community, and take legitimate sovereignty as its exercise, how in practice are we to distinguish between the general will and private wills? The establishment of the state gives it life, Rousseau tells us, but we must give it 'movement'. The exercise of sovereignty, the 'movements' of the state are matters of legislation. The creation of laws for the state must of course be based on the common good, but more specifically, the most important criteria for a given law is that it does not discriminate between the citizens. Equality, once more, is the foundation of the ideal regime:

> When I say that the object of the laws is always general, I mean that the law considers the subjects as a body and actions in the abstract, never one man as an individual, or a particular action. Thus, the law can decree that there will be privileges, but it cannot give them to particular individuals by name; the law can create several classes of citizens, even determine the qualifications which will give them the right to be in these classes, but it cannot name the specific individuals to be admitted to them; it can establish a monarchial government and hereditary succession, but it cannot elect a king or name a royal family.

In short, no function relating to an individual object belongs to the legislative power.[19]

Rousseau gives us several insights into law and government in this passage. First, we should note the importance of law's impartiality. A state must preserve equality, but only in a sense. It is not Rousseau's contention that an ideal state must be one in which every single citizen has the same amount of wealth, the same amount of property, the same amount of education, etc. As he says, there is nothing wrong with law decreeing privileges. It simply cannot decree these privileges arbitrarily to one citizen or one group of citizens over another. Most of us, I think, already take something like this to be true of just laws. So, for example, a law could decree that 'All those whose income level is below a given amount will receive support for college tuition'. But a law could never point to a specific individual simply in virtue of him being that individual and grant a similar privilege: 'Jim Delaney will receive support for college tuition' would not be a legitimate law.

Just as the state has some flexibility in the kinds of privileges it bestows on its citizens, the form of government itself has some flexibility. Rousseau says a monarchical government with rules of succession can be acceptable, provided it does not violate the rule of privileging individuals that we have just discussed. However, he also says that all legitimate governments are in fact republics. This is so because the general will is always for the will of all, and some body represents it. But the particular means of administration can vary. Nevertheless, Book Two ends with a lengthy discussion of how to preserve an ideal state. Its size can be a problem, laws are more difficult to enforce from great distances. Also, the risk of private wills overriding the general becomes greater as the number of citizens increases. On the other hand, the state must be big enough to remain stable and secure.

Book Two, then, is best understood as doing two main things. First, it sets forth a more detailed account of the philosophical framework of the general will. It explains how the general will is, and in other cases is not, represented in various state decisions. Most importantly, the notion of the general will as a collective but unified entity is put forward. Second, Book Two attempts to deal with some of the problems of the practical application of the general will. Among these are types of administration, some the aspects of legitimate law-making, and the proper size and character of the state.

Book Three

Book Three is primarily concerned with two main objectives. First, Rousseau distinguishes between sovereignty (which have seen him discuss at length in Books I and II) and *government*. Next, following political philosophers as far back as Plato and Aristotle, he discusses the three types of government: democracy, aristocracy and monarchy. Rather than claiming that one and only one of these forms of government is best, he argues instead that the appropriate form of government for a given society is ultimately determined by that society's characteristics.

To introduce the notion of government, Rousseau begins with another analogy to the individual. To accomplish any free action, he argues, an individual must be possessed of two faculties, a will and a physical power. His own example of this is walking towards an object. I must actually will myself to commit the action, that is, I must consciously decide that I want to walk towards the object; and my feet must actually take me toward the action. Both the will and the power are necessary, thus, Rousseau says, 'If a paralyzed man wills to run, and if an able bodied man wills not to run, both of them will remain where they are'.[20] We have seen throughout both the *Third Discourse* and the first two books of *The Social Contract* that Rousseau regards the state, or 'body politic', as a unified agent that is in many ways like an individual. This is the basis upon which Rousseau explains the general will and sovereignty both of which are collective. But he clearly realizes that there must be some type of mechanism in place in any state that will carry out the general will. Some states have a king, others elected officials and so on. We refer to them as the rulers, politicians and sometimes by Rousseau's own term 'the government'. He has alluded to these officials in the previous books, but almost always to emphasize that we must make sure not to confuse government with sovereignty.

However, given the analogy of the state and the individual that we have just seen in Book Three's opening, we can now understand the role of government in the state. The general will of the state is like the will of the individual. But without some sort of government in place, the state is missing the physical power or force necessary to carry out the actions that the general will desires. In this way, a state with no government of any kind would be like the paralyzed man. It may have a will, but it would lack the power to execute its will. So, properly speaking, the people represent the legislative power while the government represents the executive power.

One of the more confusing things about Rousseau's discussion is that as he speaks of these two entities, the sovereign and government, he often mentions a third, the 'subjects'. I say this is confusing because we have seen Rousseau identify the subjects themselves as the having sovereign power; how, then, can he now tell us that the subjects and the sovereign are two distinct entities? The answer is because each subject is *both* an individual with a particular will and a fraction of the whole, which is the subject of the general will. Rousseau points out in Book Two that 'There is often a great difference between the will of all and the general will'.[21] We can put the point this way. Suppose we had a thousand people living together. They would constitute a unified whole with one will, the general will, which tended toward the common good of all. However, suppose that among all of our thousand people, when each happened to view himself as an individual and exercise his private will, it just so happened that they all had a given desire in common. This would not be one will speaking to the common good of all, but rather one thousand separate wills each of which coincidentally said the same thing.

Sometimes the 'will of all' could correspond to the general will, but it need not. Consider our example of the thousand people again. Imagine that they are voting on the lowering of taxes. Each of the thousand people must cast her vote as to whether or not the state ought to do this. And finally, imagine that the vote is unanimous. Every single person votes to lower taxes. However, when they decide to vote this way, each person simply thinks 'I would like to have lower taxes'; none of them consider how the lowering of taxes might affect the state's economy, or other citizens, or the long term stability of the state. In other words, none of the subjects consider the common good at all, only their own particular wills. Ironically, it just might be that the general will *would also* dictate the lowering of taxes. Perhaps it would have long range overall benefits to the state as a whole. If this were the case, the will of all would coincidentally be aligned with the general will. But the agreement would be mere coincidence, because we could just as easily suppose that the lowering of taxes would actually hurt the state as a whole. In this case the will of all would say precisely the opposite of what the general will command.

Clearly, therefore, there is a difference between these two concepts, the subjects and the sovereign, which is I take it what Rousseau is getting at in distinguishing the general will from the will of all. Thus, it makes sense for Rousseau to discuss the sovereignty, government and the citizens as three distinct entities. Government acts as a kind of intermediary between the sovereign and the subjects:

> An appropriate agent is, therefore, needed to unite public power and put it into operation under the guidance of the general will, to assist in the communication between the state [the subjects] and the sovereign, and to do, in a way, for the public person, what the union of soul and body does for a man. This is the reason for having a government in the state, and it is inappropriately confused with the sovereign, of which it is only the minister. What, then, is government? An intermediate body established between the subjects and the sovereign for their mutual dealings, charged with the execution of the laws and with the maintenance of liberty, both civil and political.[22]

The subjects that compose the government, Rousseau calls, 'the magistrates'. The job of the magistrates is to discern the commands of the sovereign and then give orders based on those commands to the subjects. There are obviously different kinds of government that a state could have, primarily with respect to the number of magistrates that compose it. Rousseau points out the additional complication that the government itself is a collection of individuals (that is the magistrates themselves) and so it also has a will: general with regard to itself, but like all factions particular with regard to the state as a whole. Rousseau calls the will of government the 'corporate will'. This demonstrates how the job of the magistrate is more difficult than that of the average citizen. The magistrate really has three wills; the particular will of himself as an individual, the corporate will of government and the general will of the state. The corporate will, an intermediary between the will of all and the general will, will lean towards one or the other. And this will depend on the size of the state and the number of magistrates in government. The larger the number of magistrates, the closer the corporate will is to the general will. The tradeoff, however, is that as the number of magistrates increases, the efficiency of government decision making suffers. On the other hand, in a government with only one magistrate, the corporate will and the magistrates' particular will are identical and thus the furthest from the general will. However, one ruler is very efficient at making policy. So the question of 'what is the best type of government' is best answered by asking how the government can best strike a balance between reflecting the general will on one hand and efficiency on the other. This goes back to the original distinction between will and physical power, which is where Book Three began. The best type of government will depend on characteristics relative to each particular state, especially its size and population. Rousseau says:

> If the number of supreme magistrates in different states should be in inverse proportion to that of citizens, it follows that, in general, democratic government is best suited to small states, aristocracy for those of moderate size, and monarchy for large ones. This rule is derived directly from the principle, but how can we count the multitude of circumstances the can furnish expectations.[23]

Rousseau explicitly devotes subsequent chapters in Book Three to democracy, aristocracy and monarchy. Partly because I have limited space and partly because I believe these chapters to be relatively accessible on their own, I will not discuss each of them here. I will, however, mention one fundamental point that Rousseau makes with regard to democracy. While he does grant that the people themselves are in the best position to know what laws are best for them, the practical limitations make true democracy impossible. In fact, Rousseau says it has never existed. He says 'it is contrary to the natural order for the majority to govern and the minority to be governed. It is impossible to imagine that the people would constantly remain assembled to attend to public affairs, and it is evident that it could not establish committees to do so without changing the form of administration [the form of government]'.[24] Leaving the rest of the specifics with respect to democracy, aristocracy and monarchy aside, the most important elements are that the government, in whatever form it takes, is at the service of legitimate sovereignty. However, the government as an agent in itself is never to be confused with sovereignty, which always rests with the whole of the people.

Book Four

Book Four, the final Book of *The Social Contract* discusses several important notions in the maintenance of the state. Among these are voting, elections, the suspension of laws and civil religion. The discussions are practical; they build off the foundations of sovereignty, the unerring and indestructible general will and government that Rousseau lays down in the previous Books. But whereas a large portion of the previous books aimed to set up distinctions and explain how a just regime differs from an unjust one, Book Four tries to give some more concrete measures as to how such a state can sustain itself in its day to day existence. In fact, perhaps to emphasize the practical nature of his arguments, Rousseau often refers to historical examples (especially the Roman republic) to demonstrate how they either did or did not successfully let the general will reign.

Throughout the Book, Rousseau often refers to the health of the body politic, namely how in its operations it adheres to the general will. When it comes to voting, a healthy body politic will be one in which the voters base their decisions on it rather than on their individual particular wills or the particular will of some faction in society. The clearest indication that voters are doing this is the degree to which there is agreement in the voting. Since the general will always speaks in one voice, there will in theory be one objective 'right' answer for any issue: 'The more harmony reigns in the assemblies, that is, the closer opinions come to being unanimous, the more dominant, therefore, is the general will, but long debates, dissensions, and tumult proclaim the ascendancy of private interests and the decline of the state'.[25] However, unanimity in itself is not a guarantee that the general will is being exercised. Voters might be casting their votes in a uniform manner, not because they believe it to really be for the common good, but rather from a kind of coercion. They fear that if they do not fall in line, they will be punished. This danger, while it is a serious one, is fairly easy to recognize. And if that is how the voting is taking place, this is a strong indication that the state is on the decline.

One might rightfully bring up the fact that in practice, even among members of a society that truly wish to make the general will reign, there will rarely be cases of complete uniformity. So realistically, Rousseau could not possibly be telling us that we must have 100% agreement in order to pass a measure. Nothing would ever be accomplished. How much agreement must there be? Two things should be said here. First, if a given citizen is outvoted but truly believes that she has voted for the common good, the general will is no less unified. She simply must accept that what she thought the general will demanded was incorrect. Thus, she should support the body politics' decision. Disagreement, therefore, is neither a threat to the general will's expression or the freedom of the individual herself.

Second, Rousseau explains that there is not a set number on how much agreement there must be to pass a given measure. Like many other aspects of maintaining the state, the degree of agreement necessary will depend on several external factors (the size of the state, the population, etc.) Rousseau offers two general rules for regulating this process: 'the first is that the more important and serious the decisions, the closer the prevailing opinion should be to unanimity; the second is that the more hastily the matter under consideration must be decided, the smaller the prescribed majority should be'.[26]

As for elections, the means by which the magistrates are appointed, Rousseau describes two alternatives. The first is 'by lot' meaning that government officials are chosen at random. This method of election is best suited to democracy when each of the people is eligible to rule. In a legitimate democracy, ruling is a burden that falls on citizens, something like jury duty. Thus, a lottery is the best way to distribute it. The second way of performing an election is by vote, which is what we typically think of as the normal means of election; in contrast to election by lot, Rousseau refers to voting as election 'by choice'. This type of election is best suited to aristocracies, in which 'the prince chooses the prince; [and] the government preserves itself'.[27] As we saw in Book Three, however, Rousseau does not believe that a true democracy has ever existed, and so a mix between a lottery and voting is the best system. Lotteries should determine offices which simply require 'common sense', whereas voting should be done for positions that require special talents.

Following his discussion of voting and elections, Rousseau discusses two points on which I should make a brief mention. The first, the subject of Chapter 5, is the notion of the 'tribunate'. The tribunate is a special magistracy, separate from the established government. It is therefore a faculty of neither the legislative (that is the sovereignty) nor the executive (the government). The tribunate's job is to guard against the abuse of the people by the government, primarily by preserving the laws.

The second point, discussed in Chapter 6, has to do with dictatorships. One might think that Rousseau would be adamantly against dictatorships given what he has already said, and given the horrors we often associate with those who suffer at the hands of dictators. But Rousseau does not dismiss the notion of dictatorship outright. Instead, he argues that in the most desperate of circumstances, when the future of the state is at stake, the laws can be temporarily suspended and a dictator may assume power. I make mention of this to show once again that for Rousseau, there is no set formula for, nor are there explicit prohibitions on, the maintenance of a state governed by the general will.

One of the most controversial aspects of Book Four, and indeed of *The Social Contract* in general, is given in its penultimate chapter. There, Rousseau discusses civil religion. As is his custom, he begins by citing several historical examples, among them the polytheism of the ancient Greece of which he speaks relatively favourably, and Christianity which when they gained power Rousseau says resulted in the most violent despotism on earth. He later adds that 'Christian law is fundamentally more harmful than useful to the strong continuation of the state'.[28] The comments that follow echo some of the major themes of those made in *Emile*'s *Profession of Faith of the Savoyard Vicar*, which we examined in the previous chapter. There, we saw Rousseau advocate a very general religion of nature as well as a great deal of scepticism about the dogmas of particular religions (especially Catholicism). In a similar vein in *The Social Contract*, Rousseau makes a division between the 'religion of man', which parallels the religion of nature, and the 'religion of the citizen', which is merely whatever particular religion is practiced in a state:

> The former [religion of man], without temples, altars, or rites, limited to the purely inward worship of the supreme God and to the eternal duties of morality, is the pure and simple religion of the Gospel, the true theism, and what might be called the divine law. The latter [religion of the citizen], established in a single country, gives it gods, its own tutelary patrons: it has its dogmas, its rites, its outward form of worship prescribed by law; outside the single nation that practices it, this religion considers everything infidel, foreign, barbarous; it extends the duties and rights of man only as far as its altars.[29]

In addition to these two types of religion, Rousseau also adds a third, what he calls the religion of the priest. This third type is somewhat difficult to describe, but perhaps the best way to understand it is as a kind of additional religion of the citizen that runs counter to the mainstream religion of the state. Since it goes beyond the basic religion of man, the religion of nature, it is content full and has complex dogmas that carry heavy moral burdens with them. But because it is not the religion of the citizen, it will in Rousseau's words, prevent its members from being good men or good citizens. Among others, he counts Roman Catholics in this group; he dismisses this third type as being obviously bad. Whether one agrees with Rousseau or not, it is easy to see why these comments got him into trouble with the Church.

Ultimately, Rousseau gives religion a kind of subservient role within the state. As we have seen, the driving force of the legitimate state is the general will. He argues that the dogmas of civil religion should be limited, much like the religion of nature itself. First and foremost, an attitude of tolerance must be promoted among the citizens.

Iv. CONCLUSION

Rousseau's political philosophy, particularly as it relies on the notion of the general will, and the state as one unified entity, leaves one with the question of practicality. Could a state like this *really* exist? Or would an attempt to create it result in a brainwashing totalitarian regime? After the bloodshed of the French Revolution, this is a question that occupied many Rousseau scholars. These are difficult questions to answer. When we look at our own political regimes and the people within them, it seems that far more often it is the particular wills of individuals and subgroups that motivate people's actions. So one reason we might say that Rousseau's ideal regime is not practical is that, try as we might through education and other measures, human nature is such that we will *never* be able to abandon viewing ourselves first and foremost as individuals: not as parts of a whole. If we take a more optimistic view of human nature, however, one more in line with Rousseau's, we might be inclined to think his political vision could be realized. On such a view, we could say that the difficulty we have envisioning people truly seeing themselves first as citizens is due to our unfortunate historical circumstance. Just as Rousseau says Hobbes is wrong because he attributes aggression and selfishness to natural man rather than seeing them as effects of the socialization process, we might similarly say that our individualistic perspective is not natural, but acquired.

Regardless of whether the state Rousseau describes in these works is actually realizable or not, his ideas had enormous impact. They were largely influential on later thinkers such as Immanuel Kant and Karl Marx. Additionally, Rousseau was championed by leaders in the French Revolution. Thus, in addition to its purely philosophical interest, Rousseau's political thought has had far reaching historical implications.

CHAPTER 6

ROUSSEAU'S AUTOBIOGRAPHICAL WORKS

i. INTRODUCTION

Rousseau is unique among philosophers for several reasons, but one thing that sets him apart from many others is the richness and large quantity of his autobiographical works to which we have access. As I hope has been evident in some of the previous chapters of this book, Rousseau's works are not easily categorized as purely works of either autobiography, history, philosophy or literature. Rather, they are often mixed. *Emile*, for example, is simultaneously a work of fiction, a philosophical treatise and an autobiographical account. It is sometimes difficult to tell where the character of the tutor ends and Rousseau himself begins. Therefore, despite the title I have given to this chapter, I do not mean to imply that the works I will discuss here, the *Confessions*, the *Dialogues: Rousseau, Judge of Jean-Jacques* and the *Reveries of the Solitary Walker* are an exhaustive list of the works that can properly be called 'autobiographical'.

Nevertheless, for two main reasons, I think it is appropriate to group my discussion of these three works into a single chapter. First, I think that while there are certainly many other autobiographical accounts in his other works, these three, it is fair to say are first and foremost autobiographical. However, there are also many points of philosophical insight in them as well, some reiterating or re-expressing themes of previous more philosophical texts, and others that are subtly original additions to his overall thought. And, since my task in this book is primarily to explain the substance of Rousseau's philosophy, I have more or less focused my discussion of the autobiographical works on such points.

My second, and more fundamental, reason for organizing the last chapter of the book with a focus on these three works is that they are some of the last that Rousseau wrote. They also share a common theme. After two of his most principle pieces, *Emile* and *The Social Contract* were banned (primarily because of the unorthodox religious views advocated in *Emile*'s 'Profession of Faith of the Savoyard Vicar'), Rousseau became a kind of social outcast both in Paris and in his beloved homeland of Geneva. These autobiographical works are Rousseau's attempt to respond against what he sees as the public's unjust condemnation. In fact, Rousseau believes that it is more than just a case of the public misunderstanding him. He thinks that it is the result of a grand conspiracy against him, organized by those in power whose injustices his works have exposed. Much of this, it is likely, was simply in Rousseau's head, a symptom of his paranoia and growing mental instability. But they are not merely the ramblings of someone who is mentally ill. Therefore, I think it is better to treat the works impartially, to see the insights they bring to his overall thought rather than speculate about Rousseau's condition when he wrote them.

ii. THE CONFESSIONS

Published several years after his death in 1778, the *Confessions* are Rousseau's autobiography. The title is noteworthy; over 1000 years before, another famous philosopher, Saint Augustine, had given his own autobiography the same name. Augustine's is primarily a spiritual autobiography. It tells the story of his struggle to overcome his sinful nature and turn his life completely to God. The book itself is therefore written to God, and in this sense Augustine is making a confession, which is analogous to the sacrament in Roman Catholicism in which people confess their sins to a priest who then absolves them. Rousseau's *Confessions*, by contrast, are not spiritual; at least, they are not spiritual in the same way as Augustine's. Though he does talk in the opening lines of the *Confessions* of presenting himself to the 'Supreme Judge', it is clear that to a large extent the book is written to his fellow men, not to God himself. This might strike one as odd; what need does Rousseau have to make a confession to other human beings? And in what sense is simply telling others his life story a confession to begin with? I think the answers to these questions become clearer if we consider the historical and personal circumstances under which Rousseau wrote this book.

As we saw in previous chapters, two of Rousseau's major works *Emile* and *The Social Contract* were published in 1762 and then immediately banned in Paris. Rousseau was then forced to flee, going among other places to England where he stayed briefly with David Hume. After quarrelling with Hume, Rousseau left and returned to France incognito, where he began copying music for a living. He had never had all that much affection for Paris, but his works also caused him to be shunned in his beloved 'fatherland' of Geneva. By 1764, when Rousseau decided to write the *Confessions*, he felt that society itself had betrayed and misunderstood him and his work. Society, he thought, had basically accused him of sinning against them by putting forth his controversial ideas. So, Rousseau is in a sense confessing to a society that he thinks has wrongly condemned him.

When one actually reads the *Confessions*, however, it seems much more like a justification than a confession. It is not that Rousseau denies that he has made mistakes. On the contrary, much of the tone of the book is very self-deprecating. But these mistakes were in no way intentional, he tries to explain his actions and his work so as to show that whether he was successful or not, he was always making a good faith effort to contribute to the common good. The other sense in which the work's title is appropriate is the degree to which Rousseau tries to completely open himself up to the reader. The goal of the work is tell the reader everything, even the things in his life of which he is most embarrassed and ashamed. In the *Confessions*' opening lines, Rousseau announces, 'I have shown myself as I was, contemptible and vile when that is how I was, good generous, sublime when that is how I was; I have disclosed my innermost self'.[1]

The *Confessions* is a lengthy piece. In total it consists of 12 books (or chapters), and these are divided into two parts: Part One is composed of books one through six, Part Two books seven through twelve. Rather than go through the each of the 12 books individually, a task that would be beyond the scope of this section, I wish to put forth a discussion emphasizing the two points that I believe are most significant for putting the *Confessions* in the larger context of Rousseau's philosophical thought. First, I will show how some of the main themes of this thought (which we have discussed in previous chapters) are articulated in Rousseau's own personal experience. And second, I will summarize some of the interesting reflections Rousseau makes about the actual writing of his principle philosophical writings.

Of course Rousseau's philosophy cannot be itemized in a list of only a few ideas or themes, and given the richness of the *Confessions*, there are likely an infinite number of intriguing connections between it and the larger corpus of his work and thought. However, I would like to offer three particular aspects of his philosophy, aspects which were discussed at length in previous chapters and show how Rousseau develops, enhances and illustrates them in his autobiography. In short these three themes are: the notion of virtue's association with the rejection of superficial public opinion; the scepticism about the purity of morals in large urban environments and the rejection of the validity and usefulness of content laden dogma in organized religion.

In the *First Discourse*, we saw Rousseau warn that societies like ancient Athens and the modern day Paris of his day replace virtue with luxury and vain pride as they pursue advancement in the arts and sciences. In *Emile*, we saw him similarly argue that a successful moral education depended in large part in keeping the pupil isolated from the corrupting influences of these same types of societies. As we have seen in these works, Rousseau offers philosophical arguments for this claim. But in the *Confessions*, he appeals to his own personal experience. There are several examples of this, but one that is particularly poignant is in Rousseau's description of a personal 'transformation' that took place when he began ignoring public opinion. In Rousseau's words:

I was truly transformed; my friends no longer recognized me. I was no longer the timid man, easily shamed rather than modest, who dared neither to introduce himself nor to speak, whom a playful word would disconcert, whom a woman's glance would reduce to blushes. Audacious, intrepid, proud, I conducted myself everywhere with a confidence that was the more assured in that it was simple and resided in my soul rather than in any outward part.[2]

Rousseau's tone is one of feeling liberated. Once he stops caring about appealing to the manners and customs, he no longer feels constrained by them. He talks about finally 'appearing as he actually was', of finally becoming 'virtuous'. I think we can take two things away from this. First, Rousseau's own experience with such a moral transformation means that he really believed it was possible to put the lessons of works like the *First Discourse* and *Emile* into practice. And second, in keeping with the idea that the *Confessions* are an attempt to justify or explain himself and his philosophy, it is evidence that he made a genuine effort to practice what he preached.

We have observed Rousseau's scepticism about modern cities in almost all of the writings previously discussed. Recall Rousseau's praise for the pure state of nature in the *Second Discourse* and his praise in numerous works for farmers and other craftsmen that live away from big cities in rural environments. These are not claims that rest purely on philosophical speculation. Rousseau's own experience helped to shape them as well. One person in Rousseau's life who was particularly instrumental in this was a woman named Mme. de Warrens. As a youth, after he ran away from his homeland of Geneva, this woman took him in. She was instrumental in Rousseau's conversion to Catholicism (which we shall discuss below), and was, for Rousseau, a paradigm example of the simple virtue he associates with the rural environment of the countryside. He stayed with her on numerous occasions and eventually their relationship even became romantic. Whenever Rousseau speaks of her, it is with tenderness and affection, praising her virtue. But this virtue is never associated with knowledge of philosophy, or speaking well, or the sense of her having 'exquisite taste'. It is when he leaves the countryside, and goes to Paris and other cities that he encounters people with these qualities. But of course they lack virtue. So when Rousseau criticizes cities and praises rural communities, it is likely he has examples of people from his own life like Mme de Warens in mind.

Finally, it is interesting to see Rousseau's discussion of his various experiences with religion. He was born in Geneva, a Calvinist society, but as stated previously, he converted to Catholicism when he came to France in his youth. Ultimately, after the publication of the *Second Discourse*, he would make a public return to Geneva and end up converting back to Calvinism. Such conversions, basically done in order to align oneself with the particular religion of the society in which one lives, are in line with the basic responsibility of a citizen. Recall in *Emile*'s *Profession of Faith of the Savoyard Vicar* that Rousseau thinks one is obligated to practice the particular customs of whatever state religion is in place, so long as the basic moral principles of that religion provided that they are in line with the religion of nature. Recall also that in that same discussion Rousseau argues vehemently about the dogmas advocated by organized religions – especially Roman Catholicism. If one looks at Rousseau's account of his own conversion to Catholicism in the *Confessions*, it is evident how this experience could have helped shape such a view. The priests asked him a series of questions about his new faith and one of them asked if Rousseau's mother (who obviously was not herself a baptized Catholic) was damned? Rousseau, who was still very young at this point, said that he simply hoped that through God's mercy she was not. But images like this can perhaps explain why Rousseau was reluctant to praise one particular religion as the only true one, and why instead he prioritizes a general set of moral principles, the 'religion of nature'.

It is interesting to see how Rousseau's philosophy connects with his personal experiences, but the *Confessions* also provide a unique opportunity to see how he describes the actual process of how these famous works were conceived and ultimately carried out. We also get the chance to observe Rousseau's reflections on them as well as on how they were received by the public. The *Discourse on the*

Sciences and Arts is a prime example. Published in 1750, the *First Discourse*, as we saw in Chapter 2, was a response to an essay contest sponsored by the Academy of Dijon on the question of whether the advancement of the sciences and arts had tended to purify morals. In Book Eight of the *Confessions*, Rousseau tells of visiting his friend Diderot in prison in the summer of 1749. Recall that Diderot was a major figure in the enlightenment and, along with D'Alembert, was an editor on the *Encyclopédie*. Diderot had advocated atheist views, which led to his imprisonment. So during that summer, Rousseau would take the long walk to and from the prison in Vincennes every other day or so to visit him in the effort of lifting his spirits. On one of these walks Rousseau had taken a book with him, and in looking through it, he came upon the Academy of Dijon's essay contest. Rousseau describes the reaction he had upon seeing the Academy's question as nothing less than an epiphany:

> The moment I read these words I saw another universe and I became another man . . . My feelings, with incredible rapidity, had soon risen to the same pitch of fervour as my ideas. All my little passions were stifled by my enthusiasm for truth, for liberty, for virtue, and, what is most surprising of all, this ferment continued unabated in my heart for four or five years or more at as high a degree of intensity as it ever has, perhaps, in the heart of any other man.[3]

In other places, he talks of this transcendent experience of being the source and inspiration for all his works, but that the works themselves only represented a small fraction of the experience itself. Though he was wholly inspired, and would later include it among what he thought were his 'most principal works', Rousseau is somewhat critical of the *First Discourse* when he reflects on it in the *Confessions*: 'this work, although full of fire and energy, is wholly lacking in logic and order; of all those that have come from my pen, it is the weakest in its reasoning and the most deficient in proportion and harmony'.[4]

When Rousseau talks about the events that led to his writing the *Second Discourse*, he recounts a trip he took to Saint-Germain with

Thérèse and one of her friends. He describes these 7 or 8 days as one of the most pleasant times in his entire life. He spent his days in the forest contemplating the beginnings of human history. The romantic image of the forest in the *Second Discourse* is no doubt influenced by Rousseau's mediations while walking through nature. He also recounts his return to Geneva, and conversion back to Protestantism, which reignited his deep love of his homeland. Hence, the *Second Discourse* is preceded by Rousseau's dedication to Geneva, which we saw in Chapter 3 is filled with praise. Rousseau evidently thought more highly of this discourse than he did of the first one. The *Second Discourse*, unlike the first, did not win the Academy's prize, but Rousseau reacts with the following dismissal:

> . . . it [The *Second Discourse*] found in the whole of Europe only a few readers who understood it, and none of them wanted to talk about it. It had been written for the competition and so I submitted it, although I was convinced in advance that it would not win, knowing only too well that it is not for works of this kind that academics create prizes.[5]

He goes on to discuss the correspondence he had about the *Second Discourse* with Voltaire, who criticized it harshly. One notices quickly the surprise that Rousseau had about the less than warm reception this piece received from critics, a piece of which he was obviously quite proud. Once again the *Confessions* serves as a way for Rousseau to defend and explain himself.

But perhaps nowhere in the *Confessions* is more eager to defend and explain himself than in his accounts of the writing and publication of *Emile* and *The Social Contract*, both of which were published in 1762 and whose banning forced him to flee France. *Emile*, according to Rousseau, was taking particularly long at the printer's, and he began to fear that the Jesuits were plotting against him. The printing was actually even halted at one point. Finally, both *The Social Contract* and *Emile* were published with the former coming out a few months before the latter. Rousseau likens what follows to the rumblings before a storm, and talks about the need to flee: 'Seeing that I had secret and powerful enemies within the kingdom of France, I judged that, attached though I was to that country, I must leave it in order to secure my peace of mind'.[6] Once again, when one reads Rousseau's account of these events and others, it makes them strikingly personal. The *Confessions* are a curious kind of hybrid; an autobiography of an extremely interesting person, a kind of philosophical piece in their own right, and an inside look at a great philosopher's reflections on his life's work.

iii. DIALOGUES: ROUSSEAU, JUDGE OF JEAN-JACQUES

There is some ambiguity about the title of this work because the different copies that Rousseau distributed have different titles. So among scholars it is sometimes referred to as *Dialogues* and other times referred to as *Rousseau: Judge of Jean Jacques*. Rousseau intended the work as a sequel to the *Confessions*, most likely in the hope that he could be successful in the ways in which that work had failed. In the previous section dedicated to the *Confessions* we saw that Rousseau was attempting to justify and explain himself to a public that he felt misjudged both his works as well as himself personally. But the *Confessions* had not been successful, or at least they did not succeed to the degree Rousseau had hoped, in re-establishing his reputation. Some scholars believe that Rousseau's desire to try once again to justify himself to the public is part of the reason for the peculiar structure of the *Dialogues*.[7] In the *Confessions*, Rousseau is speaking directly to the public. The reader herself is the interlocutor. Thus, the reader is able to take the 'confession' and do with it what she will. And most readers, in Rousseau's eyes, either misinterpreted or simply misunderstood it. So when they were ultimately left to 'judge' Rousseau, they did so negatively.

The *Dialogues* are structured quite differently. Rousseau is still 'confessing', but he is no longer doing so by speaking directly to the reader. As the name suggests, the work is written in the form of a dialogue between two characters: 'Rousseau' and 'The Frenchman'. The *Dialogues* read much more like a play than they do a novel or formal philosophical treatise. It may be helpful to keep in mind, however, that philosophers had written in dialogue form before to convey their arguments, with Plato being the most famous example.

The work is, as we have said, best considered autobiographical. However, it is also hypothetical in an important sense. The characters of Rousseau and the Frenchmen discuss 'Jean-Jacques'. But both the character of Rousseau and the character of Jean-Jacques in the *Dialogues* are actually Jean-Jacques Rousseau himself.

The character of Jean-Jacques is the historical Rousseau, the author of the first and second *Discourses, Emile,* and *The Social Contract.* And just like the historical Rousseau (or, once again, at least as Rousseau perceives it), Jean-Jacques is despised by the public, especially the French public. The character of 'Rousseau' is more of a hypothetical construct, and an abstract one at that. The character Rousseau represents the actual historical Rousseau if he had not actually written any of the works that made him famous, or infamous. The character of Rousseau in the *Dialogues* is someone who has just arrived in France and is only aware of the character of Jean-Jacques from being familiar with his works and from his notorious public reputation. The actual Rousseau has therefore split himself into two in the *Dialogues.* This allows him to assume a position of impartiality; he is not trying 'as himself' to persuade others that his bad reputation is undeserved. But rather, he is trying to show that were he himself to look at the situation from the perspective of a third party, with no personal stake in the matter, he would conclude that the reputation was undeserved. Hence the work's other title, *Rousseau: Judge of Jean-Jacques.* He is truly judging himself, and structuring the book this way allows him to escape the pitfalls of the *Confessions.* The reader is more passive; instead of making her own judgements, the judgements are made and presented by Rousseau himself through the mouth of the Rousseau character.

The characters of Rousseau and Jean-Jacques represent Rousseau himself by splitting one subject into two. By contrast the character of the Frenchman does the opposite, merging the many voices of the public into one. The Frenchman becomes the mouthpiece of public opinion that has labelled Rousseau a monster (this is the word actually used throughout the *Dialogues*). But the Frenchman's arguments are not substantial and create the sin of favouring mere appearance over reality. The *Dialogues* are a work in three parts, simply titled the First, Second and Third Dialogue, respectively. I will discuss each briefly, pointing to what I take to be the most substantive claims in each.

The First Dialogue begins with a discussion of the charge that Jean-Jacques is a plagiarist. The Frenchman argues that Jean-Jacques, the author of the philosophical works, actually does not know music and is thus could not be the author of the popular opera the *Village Soothsayer*. Rousseau responds by saying that if Jean-Jacques did not know music, he would not have been able to write the *Dictionary of Music*. But perhaps more telling is that Rousseau says that the very act of plagiarizing shows a lack of character. How, he asks, could the author of books like *Emile*, which speak so truly of virtue and morality, be the kind of person that would do such a thing? And in a similar vein, Rousseau expands this reasoning. It applies not merely to the charge of plagiarism, but to character traits in general. Jean-Jacques is supposed to be deceitful and vile. But no one of such character could have produced the works that everyone agrees he has produced:

> . . . what I do not believe, and will never believe as long as I live, is that the *Emile*, and especially the article about taste in the fourth book, is the work of a depraved heart; that *Heloise*, and especially the letter about the death of Julie, was written by a scoundrel; that the letter to M. d'Alembert on the theater is the product of a duplicitous soul, that the summary of the *Project on Perpetual Peace* is that of an enemy of the human race, that the entire collection of writings by the same Author emanated from a hypocritical soul and evil mind and not from the pure zeal of a heart burning with love of virtue.[8]

The Frenchman responds to Rousseau's argument by saying that Jean-Jacques' works, *Emile, Julie*, etc. only speak to truth and virtue on their surface. If one reads deeply, and finds the intended hidden meaning of the text, he will find that Jean-Jacques actually advocates terrible vices. There is 'venom' in the works; for example, says the Frenchman, when one reads *Emile* carefully, he will see that Jean-Jacques very cleverly and covertly approves of murder! When

Rousseau challenges the Frenchman on this, explaining that he has read all these works very carefully and has not seen anything like this, and asks him to explain where the venom is specifically, he gets a rather startling response.

The Frenchman admits that he himself has not actually read Jean-Jacques' books. Rather, he simply has it on good public authority that these dangerous subliminal themes are part of the work. Rousseau then says that the Frenchman should go directly to the source and read Jean-Jacques' books. Furthermore he should do so carefully, reading the books objectively as if he had no idea who the author was. This, of course, is exactly what the actual Jean-Jacques Rousseau is attempting to do in the *Dialogues* with the character of Rousseau. The Frenchman agrees to do this, but only on the condition that Rousseau go to meet Jean-Jacques personally, so that he might examine him carefully in the attempt to reveal the hypocrisy; that is, to expose him as the monster he is and that the public believes him to be.

The *Second Dialogue* begins after the Frenchman has read the works of Jean-Jacques, and Rousseau has returned from his meeting with the Author. Rousseau's account of Jean-Jacques has given him a far different view of his character than that of the one depicted by the public, what is often referred to in the text as that which the 'Gentlemen' say. Among some of the characteristics falsely attributed to him, Rousseau explains that there is no doubt that Jean-Jacques does indeed know music, and that his job copying music is out of genuine necessity. He is not doing it as some charade while he is secretly rich from the publication of all his books.

The main theme of the *Second Dialogue*, however, is the moral character of Jean-Jacques himself. Rousseau does not say that he takes Jean-Jacques to actually be the most virtuous of all men; this is not surprising. For in reality, throughout almost all of his works (among the *Confessions* and *Emile* especially) whenever he refers to himself, he says that he is imperfect. He is describing men as they should be, though he realizes that he falls short. But this is a view that is quite different from that of the Gentlemen, who present Jean-Jacques as a hater of men and of virtue, as someone that is evil and proud of it. They claim that it is out of this hatred and contempt that he isolates himself from other human beings. By contrast, however, the Rousseau of the *Dialogues* characterizes Jean-Jacques as timid, weak and fearful of others. By his own admission as well as Rousseau's observation, he lacks virtue, but there was never a man who loved virtue more.

Nevertheless, the somewhat humble portrait of Jean-Jacques in the *Second Dialogue* is also supplemented not so subtly with high praise. There is a significant portion of the text dedicated to a discussion of the dangers of amour-propre. This unnatural self-love that consists in comparing oneself with others, which we examined in length particularly in *Emile*, is the source of all vices. Jean-Jacques is not at all concerned with being better than others and he cares nothing of status and luxury. The society that has condemned Jean-Jacques, however, is completely consumed by amour-propre. Recall that the character of Rousseau in the *Dialogues* is a foreigner. At the end of the *Second Dialogue*, when the Frenchman asks why we should think his testimony, that of only one individual, should be taken against that of the whole public about Jean-Jacques' character, Rousseau's response goes right to the heart of this. The society that has condemned Jean-Jacques is completely consumed by amour-propre; it is like an epidemic, a disease that has spread through them. They have joined in a kind of mob mentality against Jean-Jacques, hating him simply for the sake of hating him. And since this hate has become so ingrained, it is not surprising or suspicious that his account, though it is only based on one individual's experience, is the one that is closer to reality.

In the *Third Dialogue*, the final one, the Frenchman explains his own perspective on Jean-Jacques, having now read his works. Rousseau asks him what opinion he has formed now that he has actually read the books in question, and is surprised when the Frenchman tells him that only the vilest monster, exactly the kind described by the Gentlemen, could have produced them. But as we shall see shortly, there is an ironic twist here. He then cites passages from some of the works, among them *Emile, The Social Contract* and the *Discourse on Inequality*, which he says incriminates the author. Some of these same passages we have examined in previous chapters of this book, so I will not discuss each in detail. Generally speaking, the passages touch on Rousseau's supposed condemnation of 'Men of Letters' (namely philosophers or so-called learned individuals, 'Doctors', 'Kings, the Nobles, and the Rich', 'Women' and 'The English'). It should not be surprising that some of these groups would come under attack, for after all, Rousseau sees much of this society as a result of an illegitimate social contract that maintains an unjust system of inequality.

The Frenchman admits, however, that he had rushed to judgement before and had taken what the Gentlemen had said without any real evidence. And he then says that it is not surprising that the Gentlemen reacted as they did; Jean-Jacques is therefore not the monster they describe at all, but no one should be surprised that someone exposing these powerful groups would not be conspired against by them, which is exactly what happened. For the Frenchman has actually been quite moved by the books and has realized what Rousseau had been trying to tell him in the *First Dialogue*.

In describing the beauty of Jean-Jacques' books, the Frenchman repeatedly refers to the author's 'system'. This point is, I believe, one of the most important in the *Dialogues*. It is one of the clearest pieces of evidence from Rousseau's own mouth that his works form a coherent whole, which as I mentioned in Chapter One's introduction is a matter of debate among scholars. The themes of this whole, which we have seen articulated in previous chapters (God as a source of moral order, equality and a condemnation of superficial things), are expressed poetically when the Frenchman explains that the truth of Jean-Jacques' works will survive though he happens to live in a time when public opinion goes against them:

But this infatuation with Atheism is an ephemeral fanaticism, a product of fashion that will be destroyed by it too; and the enthusiasm with which the people surrender to it shows it is nothing but a mutiny against its conscience, whose murmur it feels with resentment. This convenient philosophy of the happy and rich who build their paradise in this world cannot long serve as the philosophy of the multitude who are the victims of their passions, and who – for lack of happiness in this life – need to find in it at least the hope and consolations of which that barbarous doctrine deprives them.[9]

Happily, the Frenchman has been converted at the end of the *Dialogues*, which ultimately is what Rousseau was hoping the book would do for its actual readers. Some try to simply dismiss the *Dialogues* as less of a philosophical work and more evidence of Rousseau's growing paranoia and lack of mental stability. There is perhaps a case to be made for this, but I believe it would be a mistake to make such a quick dismissal. This is not to say that Rousseau was not paranoid, or that his concern with what the public thought of him did not border on an unhealthy obsession. Perhaps the best evidence of this was that Rousseau tried to deposit a copy of the *Dialogues* on the Altar of Notre Dame in Paris in 1776. He wrote a brief summary of this in an epilogue to the *Dialogues* he titled 'A History of the Preceding Writing'. He ended up being unable to carry out his plan, nor to overcome the anguish he felt at not being able to offer the work to the public and to God in this way. But despite all this, the *Dialogues* themselves remain authentically Rousseau's and, as I hope I have shown in this admittedly short discussion, contribute uniquely to Rousseau's overall thought.

iv. REVERIES OF THE SOLITARY WALKER

The *Reveries of the Solitary Walker*, sometimes simply called the *Reveries*, is Rousseau's last work. I think it serves appropriately as the culmination of the autobiographical works we have discussed in this chapter. In the *Confessions*, Rousseau pleaded his case directly to the public, the readers themselves. In the *Dialogues*, he tried to give the public the voice that he thinks they would have if they truly understood him and his works. In the *Reveries*, we get the sense that Rousseau is resigned to his fate, that he will not be able to convince the public (at least in his own time) of the truth. Thus, he contemplates his solitary existence, which he enjoys on some levels but which pains him on others. Indeed he explains this difference in his mindset in the first walk:

I wrote my first *Confessions* and my *Dialogues* in a continual anxiety about ways of keeping them out of grasping hands of my persecutors and transmitting them if possible to future generations. The same anxiety no longer torments me as I write this, I know it would be useless, and the desire to be better known to men has died in my heart, leaving me profoundly indifferent to the fate of both my true writings and of the proofs of my innocence, all of which have perhaps already been destroyed for ever.[10]

Our best evidence suggests that Rousseau began writing the *Reveries* in 1776. The work is composed of ten sections or 'walks', and the process of writing took place over a period of about 2 years, with the tenth walk (which is unfinished) dated Palm Sunday of 1778. Rousseau died a few months later in July of that same year, but the *Reveries* were not published until 4 years later. Like with the *Dialogues*, some scholars are rather dismissive of the *Reveries* citing it less as an additional source of Rousseau's thought and more as evidence of his growing paranoia. However, as is my view regarding the *Dialogues*, I think the dismissal of the *Reveries* for this reason is unfortunate. We are able to glimpse how Rousseau, in his final years, continued to advocate his principal philosophical themes, and continued in his own struggle to live up to them. But at the centre of the *Reveries*, I believe, Rousseau is trying to convince his readers, and likely himself, that he no longer cares about his public image and that he has finally found peace in his solitude. Rather than go through each of the ten 'walks', I will instead try to sample various sections that I think are particularly poignant in this respect.

One of the most reccurring themes of the *Reveries* is Rousseau's continuing feeling that the society that he had only hoped to help with his works has betrayed him. There are countless passages in which he refers to his 'persecutors' and his 'enemies', which echo the discussions of the 'Gentlemen' in the *Dialogues*. However much in reality things were or were not the way Rousseau envisioned them, there is no doubt that he truly believed in a conspiracy. Because Rousseau has exposed their corruption and vice, the powerful few have convinced the masses that he is evil and misanthropic. Indeed in the opening paragraphs of the very first walk, he talks about how he never would have believed years ago that he would be painted as 'a monster, a poisoner, an assassin, that I would become the horror of the human race, the laughing-stock of the rabble . . . and that an entire generation would of one accord take pleasure in burying me alive'.[11]

In other passages, he gives accounts of the times in his life that led to the writing of his major works, which ultimately led to his public condemnation. In the third walk he discusses the deep contemplation he engaged in about the most profound philosophical questions. If he made mistakes, he never did so intentionally; he always searched for these truths with an honest heart. He describes how the conclusions he drew from these meditations ultimately became the substance of the 'Profession of Faith of the Savoyard Vicar' in Book Four of *Emile*. The reader will no doubt recall that of all his books this is the one that caused the most controversy. Rousseau says that it has been 'prostituted' and 'desecrated' by the current generation. But he nevertheless hopes that future generations will see the true meaning of it, thus vindicating the book as well as its author.

There is even a sense in which Rousseau regards himself as a kind of martyr for the human race. He begins the sixth walk by telling a story about a young crippled boy that he used to pass routinely on his walks. The boy would come over to him, and Rousseau would always give him a little money and they would engage in friendly conversation. Rousseau initially took great pleasure in this, but he eventually came to be distressed by it as it seemed more like an obligation than a gift. The boy came to expect the money from him and always made a point of addressing him by name so as to show everyone that he knew who Rousseau was. This made Rousseau realize that the boy only knew him from his public reputation, which of course was upsetting to him. This story serves as a metaphor for how Rousseau viewed society in general. By writing his books, just like giving gifts to the boy, Rousseau is doing good, which is 'the truest happiness the human heart can enjoy'.[12] But after his works became widely read, and he became a public figure, doing good became impossible just as it became impossible with the boy. He says that he became the 'universal provider for all the needy or those who claimed to be, all the tricksters in search of a dupe, and all those who used the pretext of the great influence which they pretended to attribute to me, to attempt in one way or another to take possession of me'.[13]

It is clear from the preceding that Rousseau still feels wounded, betrayed and unjustly condemned by the public. Despite this, the *Reveries* seem to be in large part an effort on the part of Rousseau to show that he actually does not feel that way at all. He talks over and over about the peace and tranquility that he has achieved in solitude. In the first walk he says that everything is finished for him on this earth, and therefore no man can do him any good or any evil, that he no longer has anything to fear but nothing to hope for either. And these reflections, which completely remove him from the rest of humanity, actually serve to give him peace. In the seventh walk, he talks about his solitary existence in the beauty of nature:

> Fleeing from men, seeking solitude, no longer using my imagination and thinking even less, yet endowed with a lively nature that keeps me from languid and melancholy apathy, I began to take an interest in everything around me, and a quite natural instinct led me to prefer those objects which were most pleasing to me.[14]

This praise of the purity of nature is followed by a condemnation of those who go beyond this enjoyment of nature's purity in the attempt to master it. Rousseau talks about man's need to scour the earth, and take its resources rather than enjoying its true blessings. If this account sounds familiar, it is because it is the roughly the same story Rousseau tells in the *Second Discourse*. But interestingly, one major point of that previous work as well as others that followed, especially *Emile*, is that the human race cannot go backward. Once we have left the state of nature for civilized society, it is too late to go back, no matter how peaceful and tranquil the life of the noble savage. But Rousseau seems to be advocating a kind of return to nature here. Of course he cannot unlearn language, nor stop from using reason. However, what he describes in the *Reveries* is a return; he is leaving society, trying to live simply, trying not to worry about the past or future. It may be that in this last of his works, Rousseau is trying as best he can to live in the pure state of nature that he had always praised.

v. CONCLUSION

My treatment of these three works is admittedly brief, and as is the case with all of Rousseau's writings, I think readers would do themselves a disservice by using the above as a substitute for reading the primary sources themselves. But my hope is that, in the examples I have chosen from the text, I have given a sense of their more noteworthy aspects.

Above all, I think there are two central elements to take away from the *Confessions, Dialogues* and *Reveries*. First, they lend further evidence to the claim that Rousseau's works, though different in scope and style, do form a coherent structure, a genuine philosophical system. Second, they give us an intensely personal perspective on Jean-Jacques Rousseau the man. For in all three, we see him arguing, almost pleading with his readers that he aimed for nothing but the common good in all his works. Whatever harms he has caused have been the result of a lack of wisdom, or a weakness of character, but never ill-intentions. In the end, he asks for acceptance and forgiveness, and wishes for the public to pity his shortcomings rather than shun him for them. Perhaps one of the more enduring things about Rousseau is that this is probably a feeling with which all of us can identify on some level.

NOTES

CHAPTER 2: PROGRESS AND MODERN SOCIETY

1 *Discourse on the Sciences and Arts*, p. 34.
2 *Ibid.*, p. 37.
3 *Ibid.*, p. 38.
4 *Ibid.*, p. 38.
5 *Ibid.*, pp. 40–1.
6 *Ibid.*, p. 43.
7 See Aristotle's *Nicomachean Ethics*, Book X, Chapters 7–10 for this discussion.
8 *Discourse on the Sciences and Arts*, p. 48.
9 *Ibid.*, p. 50.
10 *Ibid.*, p. 53.
11 *Ibid.*, p. 55.
12 *Ibid.*, p. 55.
13 *Ibid.*, p. 58.
14 *Ibid.*, p. 63.
15 D'Alembert. *Encyclopédie*. Available in *The Collected Writings of Rousseau*, Vol. 10, p. 244.
16 *Letter to D'Alembert*, pp. 263–4.
17 *Ibid.*, p. 309.
18 *Julie or the New Heloise*, p. 3.
19 *Ibid.*, p. 48.
20 *Ibid.*, p. 410.

CHAPTER 3: THE STATE OF NATURE AND HUMAN HISTORY

1 *Second Discourse*, p. 78.

2   We shall see Rousseau argue for this claim at length in later works
    on political philosophy.
3   *Ibid.*, p. 87.
4   *Ibid.*, p. 88.
5   *Ibid.*, p. 89.
6   *Ibid.*, p. 229.
7   *Ibid.*, p. 91.
8   *Ibid.*, p. 102. This passage follows the preface, and is included in a
    brief introductory section that precedes the first part of the *Second
    Discourse.*
9   Hobbes, Thomas. *De Cive* or *The Citizen* (S. P. Lamprecht, ed.).
    Westport, CT: Greenwood Press (1982), pp. 21–2.
10 *Ibid.*, p. 129.
11 *Second Discourse*, pp. 95–6.
12 Ohagen, Timothy. *Rousseau.* London and New York: Routledge
    (1999), p. 37.
13 *Second Discourse*, p. 104.
14 *Ibid.*, p. 105.
15 *Ibid.*, p. 106.
16 *Ibid.*, p. 107.
17 *Ibid.*, p. 110.
18 *Ibid.*, p. 113.
19 *Ibid.*, p. 105.
20 *Ibid.*, p. 116.
21 This is the view that being free consists in the ability of an agent to 'do
    otherwise' in a given situation.
22 *Ibid.*, p. 113.
23 *Ibid.*, p. 114.
24 *Ibid.*, p. 114.
25 *Ibid.*, p. 114.
26 *Ibid.*, p. 115.
27 *Ibid.*, p.116.
28 Aristotle. Metaphysics I . . . W. D. Ross Translation.
29 *Second Discourse*, p. 117.
30 *Ibid.*, p. 124.
31 *Ibid.*, p. 128.
32 *Ibid.*, p. 130.
33 *Ibid.*, p. 131.
34 *Ibid.*, pp. 131–2.
35 *Ibid.*, p. 127.
36 *Ibid.*, p. 140.
37 *Ibid.*, p. 141.
38 O'Hagan, Timothy (1999), *Rousseau.* New York, NY: Routledge Press.

39   *Ibid.*, p. 143.
40   *Ibid.*, p. 146.
41   *Ibid.*, p. 151.
42   *Ibid.*, p. 151.
43   *Ibid.*, p. 152.
44   *Ibid.*, p. 154.
45   *Ibid.*, p. 157.
46   *Ibid.*, p. 159.
47   *Ibid.*, p. 162.
48   *Ibid.*, p. 172.
49   *Ibid.*, pp. 180–1.

CHAPTER 4: PHILOSOPHY OF EDUCATION

1   I refer to the 2000 Everyman Press edition, which is the one I quote throughout.
2   *Emile*, p. 6.
3   *Ibid.*, pp. 7–8.
4   *Ibid.*, pp. 23–4.
5   *Ibid.*, p. 40.
6   *Ibid.*, p. 56.
7   *Ibid.*, p. 66.
8   *Ibid.*, p. 145.
9   *Ibid.*, p. 148.
10   *Ibid.*, p. 173.
11   *Ibid.*, pp. 177–8.
12   *Ibid.*, p. 180.
13   *Ibid.*, p. 184.
14   The Barbara Folxley translation from which I am quoting in this book translates *amour de soi* simply as 'self-love.' It translates *amour-propre* as 'selfishness' to distinguish the two terms. However, following the majority of Rousseau scholars writing in English, I have chosen to simply leave the terms in the original French.
15   *Emile*, p. 208.
16   *Ibid.*, p. 208.
17   *Ibid.*, p. 211.
18   For an excellent account of these discussions of *amour-propre*, see 'Rousseau on *Amour-Propre*' by NJH Dent and Timothy O'Hagan, as well as *Rousseau's Theodicy of Self-Love*, by Fredrick Neuhouser.
19   *Ibid.*, p. 224.
20   *Ibid.*, p. 258.
21   *Ibid.*, p. 264.
22   *Ibid.*, p. 277.

23 *Ibid.*, p. 277.
24 *Ibid.*, p. 277.
25 *Ibid.*, p. 278.
26 See Thomas Aquinas' *Summa Theologica*: First Part, a, Question 2, Article 3.
27 *Emile*, p. 282.
28 *Ibid.*, p. 281.
29 *Ibid.*, p. 283.
30 *Ibid.*, p. 304.
31 *Ibid.*, p. 305.
32 *Ibid.*, p. 292.
33 *Ibid.*, p. 311.
34 *Ibid.*, p. 276.
35 *Ibid.*, p. 321.
36 *Ibid.*, p. 326.
37 *Ibid.*, p. 363.
38 *Ibid.*, p. 362.
39 *Ibid.*, p. 383.
40 *Ibid.*, p. 388.
41 *Ibid.*, p. 392.
42 *Ibid.*, p. 412.
43 *Ibid.*, p. 466.
44 *Ibid.*, p. 493.
45 *Ibid.*, p. 524.

CHAPTER 5: POLITICAL PHILOSOPHY

1 *Discourse on Political Economy*, p. 60.
2 See Aristotle's *Politics*, Book I, Chapters 3–4.
3 *Discourse on Political Economy*, p. 60.
4 See the opening lines of the Introduction in the *Leviathan* for Hobbes' version of the political state as an individual human body.
5 *Discourse on Political Economy*, p. 61.
6 *Ibid.*, p. 62.
7 *Ibid.*, p. 64.
8 *Ibid.*, p. 66.
9 *Ibid.*, p. 73.
10 *Ibid.*, p. 76.
11 *Ibid.*, pp. 81–2.
12 *Ibid.*, p. 82.
13 *On Social Contract*, p. 85.
14 *Ibid.*, p. 92.
15 *Ibid.*, p. 93.

16 *Ibid.*, p. 95.
17 *Ibid.*, p. 99.
18 *Ibid.*, p. 102.
19 *Ibid.*, p. 106.
20 *Ibid.*, p. 118.
21 *Ibid.*, p. 100.
22 *Ibid.*, p. 119.
23 *Ibid.*, p. 125.
24 *Ibid.*, p. 124.
25 *Ibid.*, p. 150.
26 *Ibid.*, p. 152.
27 *Ibid.*, p. 153.
28 *Ibid.*, pp. 168–9.
29 *Ibid.*, p. 169.

CHAPTER 6: ROUSSEAU'S AUTOBIOGRAPHICAL WORKS

1 *Confessions*, p. 5.
2 *Ibid.*, p. 407.
3 *Ibid.*, p. 342.
4 *Ibid.*, p. 343.
5 *Ibid.*, p. 380.
6 *Ibid.*, p. 568.
7 For an excellent example, see Roger Masters' in introduction to the *Dialogues* in the *Collected Writings of Rousseau*, which to this point is the only English translation of the *Dialogues* available.
8 *Dialogues*, pp. 24–5.
9 *Ibid.*, p. 241.
10 *Reveries of the Solitary Walker*, p. 34.
11 *Ibid.*, p. 28.
12 *Ibid.*, p. 94.
13 *Ibid.*, p. 94.
14 *Ibid.*, p. 112.

BIBLIOGRAPHY AND SUGGESTIONS
FOR FURTHER READING

i. WORKS OF ROUSSEAU CITED IN THIS BOOK

I have on occasion made references to some of Rousseau's works to which I have not devoted explicit sections of this book. However, I have chosen the following ten as the most fundamental for someone approaching Rousseau for the first time. Though not yet completed, there is a Collected Writings of Rousseau that is becoming the standard for scholars working in English. However, my citations in this book (with the exceptions of the *Letter to D'Alembert*, *Julie* and *Dialogues: Rousseau, Judge of Jean-Jacques*) are taken instead from other editions. The reason for this is twofold. First, if the reader is approaching Rousseau as part of an undergraduate or high school level course, it is more likely that they will be using these editions than the Collected Writings Series. Second, on a purely practical level, if one is looking to purchase stand alone editions of particular works, it would be more economical to purchase one of these editions rather than volumes of the Collected Writings, which include a great deal of correspondence and other supporting materials that, while valuable, are probably not of too much use to someone 'starting with Rousseau'. The citations to Rousseau in this book are therefore taken from the following editions:

Citations from the *Discourse on the Sciences and Arts* and the *Discourse on the Origin of Inequality Among Men* are taken from:

Rousseau, Jean-Jacques (1969), 'The first and second discourses', in Roger Masters (ed.), *Judith Masters and Roger Masters*. trans. New York, NY: St. Martin's Press.

Citations from the *Letter to D'Alembert* are taken from:

Rousseau, Jean-Jacques (2004), Roger Masters and Christopher Kelly (eds), *Collected Writings of Rousseau Vol. 10*. Hanover and London: University Press of New England.

Citations from *Julie or the New Heloise* are taken from:

Rousseau, Jean-Jacques (1997), Roger Masters and Christopher Kelly (eds), *Collected Writings of Rousseau Vol. 6*. Hanover and London: University Press of New England.

Citations from the *Emile* are taken from:

Rousseau, Jean-Jacques (2000), *Emile*. Barbara Foxley, trans. London: Everyman Press.

Citations from the *Discourse on Political Economy* and the *Social Contract* are taken from:

Rousseau, Jean-Jacques (1988), Alan Ritter (ed.), *Rousseau's Political Writings*. Julia Conaway Bondanella, trans. New York and London: W.W. Norton and Company.

Citations from the *Confessions* are taken from:

Rousseau, Jean-Jacques (2000), Patrick Coleman (ed.), *The Confessions*. Angela Scholar, trans. New York: Oxford University Press.

Citations from *Dialogues: Rousseau, Judge of Jean Jacques* are taken from:

Rousseau, Jean-Jacques (1990), Roger Masters and Christopher Kelly (eds), *The Collected Writings of Rousseau Vol. 1*. Hanover and London: University Press of New England.

Citations from the *Reveries of the Solitary Walker* are taken from:

Rousseau, Jean-Jacques (1979), *Reveries of the Solitary Walker*. Peter France, trans. London: Penguin Books.

ii. OTHER WORKS BY ROUSSEAU

Though the works I have chosen to focus on in this book are, in my opinion, the most appropriate to understand Rousseau's most fundamental philosophical ideas, Rousseau produced a great many others. Below is a list of those I think noteworthy, and where appropriate, a very brief description:

'The Village Soothsayer' (1753), Rousseau's opera: it was performed in France and widely successful.

'Narcissus or the lover of himself' (1753), A play written by Rousseau.

'Letter on French music' (1753), A critical analysis of French music.

'Letter to Christopher de Beaumont, Archbishop of Paris' (1763), Rousseau's attempt to justify the natural religion advocated in *Emile* that had been publically condemned.

'Letters Written from the Mountain' (1764), Rousseau's response to criticisms of the *Social Contract*.

'Dictionary of Music' (1767).

'Considerations on the Government of Poland' (1782), Rousseau's unfinished commentary on the government of Poland.

In addition to these works, much of Rousseau's correspondence with other philosophers, authors and political and religious figures is also available. The best comprehensive source for these interesting pieces is the Collected Writings of Rousseau.

iii. SECONDARY LITERATURE ON ROUSSEAU

There is an enormous amount of secondary literature on Rousseau. It would of course be impossible to list all of the works available to those looking to pursue Rousseau's philosophy, literature and music in more depth. Nevertheless, below is a selection of books and articles that I believe represents a good sample of some of the better regarded and accessible materials that might be helpful in this respect. In large part, these along with the primary texts of Rousseau himself, have shaped my understanding of Rousseau and this book.

Axinn, Sidney (1981), 'Rousseau "versus" Kant on the concept of man'. *Philosophical Forum*, 12, 348–355.

Bien, Joseph (1977), 'On nature and destiny in Jean Jacques Rousseau's "Discourse on Inequality" '. *Man and World*, 10, 466–473.

Canovan, Margaret (1987), 'Rousseau's two concepts of citizenship', in E. Kennedy and S. Mindus (eds), *Women and Western Political Philosophy*. Brighton, UK: Wheatshift.

Cassirer, Ernst (1963), *Rousseau, Kant, and Goethe*, trans. P. Gay. Bloomington, IN: Library of Liberal Arts Press.

Cassirer, Ernst (1954), *The Question of Jean-Jacques Rousseau*, trans. P. Gay. New York: Columbia University Press.

Cell, Howard and Macadam, James (1988), *Rousseau's Response to Hobbes*. New York: Lang Press.

Cooper, Laurence D. (1999), *Rousseau and Nature: The Problem of the Good Life*. University Press, PA: Penn State University Press.

Delaney, James (2006), *Rousseau and the Ethics of Virtue*. London: Continuum Press.

Dent, N.J.H. (1988), 'The basic principle of Emile's education'. *Journal of Philosophy of Education*, 22, 139–149.

Dent, N.J.H. (1988), *Rousseau*. Oxford: Blackwell Press.

Dent, Nicholas (2005), *Rousseau*. London: Routledge Press.

Dent, N.J.H. (1998), 'Rousseau on amour-propre'. *Aristotelian Society*, 72, 57–73.

DeOlaso, Ezequiel (1988), 'The two skepticisms of the Savoyard Vicar', in Richard Watson (ed.), *The Skeptical Mode in Modern Philosophy*. Dordrecht: Kluwer Press.

Emberley, Peter (1986), 'Rousseau versus the Savoyard Vicar: the profession of faith considered', *Interpretation*, 14, 299–329.

Gourevitch, Victor (1988), 'Rousseau's Pure State of Nature'. *Interpretation*, 16, 23–59.

Hall, John (1973), *Rousseau*. Cambridge: Schenkman Publishing.

Hartle, Ann (1983), *The Modern Self in Rousseau's Confessions: A Reply to Saint Augustine*. Notre Dame, IN: University of Notre Dame Press.

Hiley, David (1990), 'The individual and the general will: Rousseau reconsidered'. *History of Philosophy Quarterly*, 7, (2), 159–178.

John, G. (1981), 'The moral education of Emile'. *Journal of Moral Education*, 11, 18–31.

Jones, W.T. (1987), 'Rousseau's general will and the problem of consent'. *Journal of the History of Philosophy*, 25, 105–130.

Kain, Philip (1990), 'Rousseau, the general will, and individual liberty'. *History of Philosophy Quarterly*, 315–334.

Losco, Joseph (1988), 'Rousseau on the political role of the family'. *History of Political Thought*, 9, 91–110.

MacIntyre, Alasdair (1983), Preface to *The Modern Self in Rousseau's Confessions*. Notre Dame, IN: Notre Dame University Press.

Marshall, Terrence (1978), 'Rousseau and Enlightenment'. *Political Theory*, 6, 421–455.

Montoya-Saenz, Jose (1993), 'Aristotle and Rousseau on Men and Citizens'. *Philosophical Inquiry*, 21, 65–78.

Neuhouser, Fedrick (2008), *Rousseau's Theodicy of Self-Love: Evil Rationality, and the Drive for Recognition*. New York: Oxford University Press.

Nichols, Mary (1985), 'Rousseau's novel education in the "Emile"'. *Political Theory*, 13, 535–558.

O'Hagan, Timothy (1999), *Rousseau*. New York, NY: Routledge Press.

O'Hagan, Timothy (1999), *Rousseau The Arguments of Philosophers*. New York, NY: Routledge Press.

O'Hagan, Timothy and Dent, N.J.H. (1999), 'Rousseau on "amour-propre": on six facets of "amour-propre"'. *Proceedings of the Aristotelian Society*, 99, 91–107.

Perkins, Merle (1974), *Jean Jacques Rousseau: On the Individual and Society*. Lexington: The University Press of Kentucky.

Putterman, Ethan (1999), 'The role of public opinion in Rousseau's conception of property'. *History of Political Thought*, 20, 417–437.

Riley, Patrick (1986), *The General Will Before Rousseau: The Transformation of the Divine Into the Civic*. Princeton: Princeton University Press.

Riley, Patrick (ed.) (2001), *The Cambridge Companion to Rousseau*. Cambridge: Cambridge University Press.

Simon, Julia (1995), 'Natural freedom and moral autonomy: Emile as parent, teacher, and citizen'. *History of Political Thought*, 16, 21–36.

Simpson, Matthew (2007), *Rousseau: A Guide for the Perplexed*. London: Continuum Press.

Starobinski, Jean (1988), *Rousseau*. Chicago: University of Chicago Press.

Wolker, Robert (1995), *Rousseau*. Oxford: Oxford University Press.

Wolker, Robert (1995), *Rousseau and Liberty*. Manchester: Manchester University Press.

INDEX